Shopping Smart

SHOPPING SMART

The only consumer guide
you'll ever need

by JOHN STOSSEL

G. P. PUTNAM'S SONS   NEW YORK

DESIGNED BY HELEN BARROW

LIBRARY OF CONGRESS CATALOGING IN PUBLICATION DATA
Stossel, John.
         Shopping smart.

         1. Consumer education. 2. Shopping—United States.
3. Commercial products—United States. I. Title.
TX335.S785 1980   640.73   80-14936
ISBN 0-399-12511-6

PRINTED IN THE UNITED STATES OF AMERICA

For help in writing this book, I would like to thank
Margaret Busch, Dan Danser, Martha Esposito, Tom Guinzberg,
Ronald Guttman, Bob Lange, Richard Liebner,
Mary Anne Madden, Elena Mannes, Dr. Alan Meyers,
Elaine Pappas, Alice Pifer, Donna Poydinecz-Conley,
Abby Rockmore, Otto Stossel, and Anne Stossel.

*To Judy Kuriansky,
for all her help*

Contents

Shopping Smart

Buying a Car

NEW CARS

"Buying a car is partly a sexual act." So says Ernest Dichter, a psychologist who specializes in product packaging. Big corporations pay him gobs of money to devise eye-catching boxes for Pringles, California Prunes, cars and so on. When Ford Motor Company paid Dichter to find out why the Edsel was failing, he told them it was partly sexual: "The Edsel is a castrated car. People buy cars to feel more virile, hence all the aggressive animal names (Cougar, Mustang, Stingray). We say, 'Give it to her' when we tell someone to accelerate quickly . . . it's about power . . . penetration. The Edsel failed because it didn't fulfill this fantasy."

I find this hard to swallow. I've always thought I bought cars because I wanted the cheapest way to get home from work without a breakdown, in comfort, and with enough glove-compartment room for magazines and junk food. I can't help you with your sexual identity, but for practical information, read on.

PICKING THE DEALER

Nobody rates dealers, so I suggest you select by geography. Shop the Yellow Pages and choose several dealers nearby. You want *several* because you're going to play them off against each other. You want *nearby* because your dealer handles all repairs under the warranty. You might as well make your repair trips convenient.

Once you've narrowed the choice, call the Better Business Bureau. The Bureau's ratings are crude: they don't say a dealer is good, medium or poor. But they sometimes say a dealer "does not meet our standards." That's a serious warning; it means there were significant complaints that the Bureau could not satisfactorily resolve. Probably, the BBB wrote to the dealer, asking, "What about complainant A's allegations that you would not repair. . . ." The dealer ignored the letters or told the BBB to shove it. Unfortunately, most people don't bother to report problems to the BBB, so there are plenty of bad businesses with good ratings. I don't think there are many good businesses with bad ratings. If you hear of a bad rating, that's trouble.

PICKING THE CAR

Consumer Reports probably gives the best advice on picking cars. Incognito, the magazine buys the cars (so the manufacturers can't provide a specially prepared car) and gives detailed ratings. Sample:

> "Ford Granada. Comfort: good in front . . . fair in rear. Awkward for short driver. Ride: good. Effective climate control. Strong acceleration . . . numb power steering is perhaps the worst feature . . . newer, lighter Fairmont, Zephyr are better values."

For more opinions, try *Motor Trend* or *Car and Driver*.

Some people think *Consumer Reports* goes overboard when it comes to safety. You decide. The magazine rated Chrysler's top-selling Plymouth Horizon and Dodge Omni "not acceptable." The reason: At 55 mph, if you jerked the steering wheel (as if to avoid a squirrel) and kept your hands off the wheel, the car would swerve around. Other cars quickly return to their original course. *Consumer Reports* held a news conference to announce this. They played a film that showed Omni and Horizon models swerving around.

Chrysler was very public-relations smart about this. They heard about the news conference and crashed it. First they stood nervously in the back of the room. Then I asked the *Consumer Reports* spokesman if he'd let the Chrysler people reply. He said, "All right, when I'm through."

Chrysler argued that the *Consumer Reports* test was stupid because in real life, people don't jerk the wheel and *then let go of it.* Chrysler, wise to the influence of television, had even quickly prepared press releases and their own film illustrating their point. So, that night on the news, both points of view were presented. It's rare that a company gets its side aired so quickly. Usually, when a company is publicly attacked, lawyers run around ordering employees not to comment. As a result, the attack goes unanswered, the company's product is damaged, and company officers look like jerks. Sometimes they recover from their panic and issue a pompous statement a day or two later, which gets buried on page 48 of the newspaper. Chrysler, however, got its arguments on the air that night and into the papers immediately, and thereby diluted much of *Consumer Reports'* attack. Omni and Horizon are selling fine.

Later, the U.S. Department of Transportation investigated the steering complaint and decided it was not worth pursuing. Chrysler has since fixed the problem (though it never admitted there was a problem).

SETTING THE PRICE

It's a game. The automaker prints a meaningless sticker price in case someone is dumb enough to walk in the showroom and simply pay it. The rest of us bargain. (Some exceptions: Sellers of Stingrays, Maseratis, Mercedeses, Porsche-Audis and some other specialty cars do not discount.)

For $15.00 CAR/PUTER (1603 Bushwick Ave., Brooklyn, New York 11207) will tell you what the dealer paid for the car. But that's of limited use because you still don't know how much he needs to tack on for overhead, profit, etc. The best move is to bring one dealer's price to the next dealer, and back, and let them auction you off. Lowest price wins. Sometimes you can bargain the price down as much as $1,000 below sticker price.

When comparing prices, don't be fooled by "twin" cars. Today automakers often produce several models simply by putting different cosmetics on identical cars. For example, a Chevy Impala has the same body as a Buick LeSabre, a Pontiac Catalina and an Olds 88. Only superficial features are different. This gives General Motors (GM) four "different" cars to sell. Other twins are:

CHRYSLER:
Dodge Aspen/Plymouth Volaré
Dodge Diplomat/Chrysler le Baron
Plymouth Horizon/Dodge Omni
Chrysler Cordoba/Dodge Mirada
Dodge Colt Hatchback/Plymouth Champ
Dodge St. Regis/Chrysler New Yorker/Chrysler Newport
    Plymouth Grand Fury
Dodge Challenger/Plymouth Sapporo

FORD:
Ford Fairmont/Mercury Zephyr
Ford Granada/Mercury Monarch

GENERAL MOTORS:
Olds Cutlass/Buick Century/Pontiac LeMans/Chevy Malibu
Olds Omega/Pontiac Phoenix/Chevy Citation/Buick Skylark
Olds '88/Pontiac Catalina/Buick LeSabre/Chevy Caprice
& Impala
Olds Cutlass Supreme/Buick Regal/Chevy Monte Carlo

When comparing prices, you may want to treat these "twins" as identical cars.

Another pricing trick: The dealer quotes you a very low price (he has no intention of selling the car for that). You shop around, and of course no one beats that price. You return, ready to buy, and he says, "Oh, that was a mistake. It's $200 more." You're tired of shopping, so you buy.

Moral: If you are offered a low price, get it in writing. Even that isn't foolproof. Sometimes the dealer will say the salesman "didn't have the authority to make that offer." Get the sales *manager* to put it in writing.

If you don't want to bargain, CAR/PUTER (1603 Bushwick Ave., Brooklyn, New York 11207 PHONE: 800-221-4001, or if you are in New York, 212-455-2500) will arrange for a dealer to sell you the car for no more than $150 over the dealer's cost. You pay CAR/PUTER $15.00 plus 2% (that's $140 on a $7,000 car). It's a good deal. The dealer is willing to take the small profit because CAR/PUTER does most of the work. One disadvantage: the dealer may not be close to your home, so warranty service may be difficult. Also, if there's a lot of demand for the car you want, CAR/PUTER may not be able to get it for you because dealers get much more for those cars by selling them directly.

WHEN TO BUY

"Buy at year's end!" used to be the rule. True, dealers lower prices at the season's end because they've got to dump cars to make room for new models. But today, automakers raise prices several times during the year, so the year-end discount doesn't save you as much. Also, a new car starts depreciating as soon as it leaves the showroom. Sell it the next year, and you've had one year's use of the car, but two year's depreciation loss. *Do* buy at the end of a *month,* however. Car dealers have their employees on quota systems ("Sell ten cars or you're fired") and bonuses ("Sell fifteen and you get a $500 bonus"). Hence, there's extra fierce discounting at the end of the month, when one more sale might mean either a bonus or not being fired.

You also increase your bargaining power by shopping in bad weather, or over holidays. A dealer's desperate to sell when a Christmas ice storm has kept the showroom empty of customers.

OPTIONS

Dealers push options because that's where they make their biggest profit. Not all are what they seem. Consider:

Undercoating: It sounds like something that seals your car and prevents rust. According to *Consumer Reports,* however, undercoating's purpose is to reduce noise and the undercoating already put on at the factory is enough to do that. The rust-proofing ability of undercoating sprayed on by dealers is "questionable," and adds a gas-eating 40 pounds to the car.

Tinted windows: Yes, they cut some glare, but they also make it more difficult to see at night. Sunglasses are cheaper.

Extra options often mean extra weight, and extra things to repair. *Headlamps that recede* behind covers may look nice, but they also jam and freeze shut. *Power windows* add weight and provide one more thing for your mechanic to be bewildered about. *Hatchbacks* (a cross between a sedan and a station wagon) are very popular now, but *Consumer Reports* points out two problems that you might not have thought of: Hatchback roofs slope down at the back "so that tall cargo must be pushed inconveniently far forward into the car before the hatch can close and you lose the use of the rear seat for passengers." Also with a hatchback (unlike inside a trunk), the cargo is visible; that tempts thieves.

TAKING DELIVERY

Never accept the car without a test drive. If the test drive reveals problems, don't pay until the problems are fixed. Later in this chapter, I talk about "lemons," and how, once you've got a lemon, there's little you can do about it. *Now* is the time to do something about it, *before you've paid*. After you pay, the dealer has little interest in you; you are just another pain-in-the-neck customer demanding warranty work. (Dealer: "I hate warranty work. It ties up my mechanics. I make little if any profit on it . . . and it takes forever for the manufacturer to reimburse me.")

Before you pay, however, you've got leverage. The dealer has this $5,000 monster cluttering up his lot. He wants the car out and your money in. To get it, he'll do the work you ask for and do it fast.

Watch out for "dealer prep." GM, Ford, Chrysler and most European automakers reimburse their dealers for preparation charges. It's included in the sticker price. If you pay the dealer, then you're paying "dealer prep" twice. You should pay the dealer only if you've asked him for some extra preparation, like undercoating.

FINANCING

Many car buyers bargain their brains out, running back and forth from dealer to dealer, bargaining hard to get another $20 to $30 off the purchase price. Then, they throw their savings away by not doing similar price shopping for the car loan.

If you want to finance the car, the dealer will say, "Oh, no sweat, we'll get you financing." Sure they will, at an interest rate that will make them more money than they would have made if they'd sold you all those ridiculous options you turned down. Look at the difference the interest rate makes: On a typical, 4-year, $8,000 loan, if I finance the car at 12.08%, the interest costs me $2,328 over 4 years. If I finance at 11.40%, it costs me $1,999. I save $329 by shopping for my loan, on just a ½% difference!

Suggestion: First try your credit union, then the AAA (Automobile Association of America), if you're a member. Then try a bank. All will probably be cheaper than your dealer. Not all banks are equally cheap, however. A Federal Reserve System survey taken on one August day found bank rates varying from 10% to 13.38%.

Samples:

New England Merchant (Boston)	10%
State St. Bank & Trust (Boston)	11%
Union Center (New Jersey)	10¼%
First Jersey National (New Jersey)	11½%
Chemical Bank (New York City)	13.38%

In California, Bank of America had the nerve to advertise LOW BANK RATES when their rates were 3% *higher* than other banks charged. San Francisco's District Attorney got on their case and got the bank to lower its rates, and pay a $275,000 settlement. But, if banks don't advertise their rates, there's nothing illegal about charging high interest. The point: Shop around.

Some dealers and banks may tell you the law says you must buy accident and credit-life insurance if you take out a car loan. Bull. State laws don't require it; the insurance is optional. I don't recommend that you buy either policy. All credit-life insurance does is cover the balance of your car payments in case you die before you've paid off the loan. But if you're dead, what do you care? Okay, maybe you don't want your heirs saddled with your debts; but if they don't need your car, wouldn't it be simpler to just let the car be repossessed if you die? Morbid stuff. Don't pay the high premiums.

USED CARS

Despite all the used car jokes, used cars are probably better buys than new cars. That's because new cars lose so much of their value immediately after leaving the showroom. Buy later, and you let someone else pay the heavy depreciation. Yes, repairs cost more with used cars, but even unusual repairs will probably cost you less than a new car's depreciation loss.

PRICE

Don't pay the price on the windshield; that's simply what the dealer would like to get. You should bargain. So that you know the *approximate* value of the car, consult the National Auto Dealers Official Used Car Guide or the Kelley Blue Book. If the dealer won't show you his copy, a bank or loan company will be happy to show you theirs.

CHOOSING THE CAR

Forget the odometer reading. Yes, there is a law that makes it illegal to set the mileage back, but resetting is still done, and there's no practical way you can detect it. (But there are clues: do ten other cars in the lot have the same mileage reading?) Besides, mileage isn't that important. A 100,000-mile car driven mostly on highways and maintained regularly is a better buy than a 50,000-mile car used by a nervous, stop-and-go driver, who didn't bring it in for checkups.

Performance is still the best test, so demand a test drive. Don't worry about being pushy—dealers expect you to demand test drives; they think you're a fool if you don't. Any dealer who resists a test drive clearly has something to hide.

Drive at different speeds during the test drive since some defects are apparent at one speed but not at another. Note the exhaust; heavy smoke indicates problems. Go back and forth a few times; the gears should slip smoothly from forward to reverse. Appearance won't tell you much: dealers are experts at hiding defects. (Some even spray cars with an aerosol scent called "new car smell.") However, a major accident is hard to disguise: put your cheek against the car and look down the side.

Ripples in the metal or slight differences in paint shades indicate wounds that have been painted over.

Another indicator of serious internal damage is "crabbing." Have someone stand behind the car as you drive away; if the car body doesn't seem to point exactly in the direction you're going, that car has been very, very sick.

Tires give you still another warning. If the tread is uneven (one part is more worn than another), something is going wrong inside the car.

I could list other tests, but they're more complicated, and frankly, I wonder how useful it is for us to try to out-mechanic the dealer. If you are like me, you don't know much about car mechanics. A smart dealer can feed us a line of bull to explain any defect. So the best test is to take the car to a real mechanic. Do it on your test drive (make an appointment in advance). For about $30, an independent garage will examine the car and tell you more than the dealer ever will.

Another good test is to talk to the car's previous owner. He can tell you the *real* mileage, whether he had a major accident, whether he maintained the car properly, and so forth. He has no reason to lie since he has no financial interest in the sale. Maybe he'll tell you that the car was such a horrible lemon, he feels lucky to have sold it. The dealer may not want to tell you who the previous owner is; he may tell you he doesn't know. You then can tell him he's full of it; the law says he must have the previous owner's name. The law does not say he has to tell you the name, however. But if he won't, doesn't that make you think he has something to hide? If a dealer has purchased the used car from another dealer or a finance company, he may not yet have the owner's name. It will take him a while to get it, but he can get it. If, after pressure, he still won't tell you the former owner's name, note the license plate and call that State's Department of Motor Vehicles. In some states, the Motor Vehicles Department will tell you who used to own the car.

MONEY-SAVING TIPS

You'll get a better deal buying the slightly "different" car, the car fewer people want. An ugly colored car, for example, may be cheap enough that you could pay to have it repainted and still come out ahead. You may get a better price if you buy a luxury car without air-conditioning because most luxury-car buyers want air-conditioning. Since most buyers want low-mileage cars, you get better deals buying well-maintained, high-mileage cars.

AVOID high-powered "muscle" cars and other teenage hot rods. Imagine what a tough life these cars had before they got to you. Also, these cars are expensive because a lot of the kids who buy them can't afford new cars, so they drive up the "muscle" prices on the used car market.

AVOID cars with lots of fancy options, like power windows. The extra options attract buyers and keep the price up. Get them in a used car and you've mainly got extra things that break down.

If you have time, wait. Watch the car lot. If there's a car that has been sitting unsold for a month or two, the dealer may be so desperate to get rid of it that he'll give you an extra good bargain.

WHERE TO BUY

New car dealers sell the best used cars (they unload their worst trade-ins onto used car dealers). New car dealers give the best warranties. However, they also charge the most for their used cars.

Used car dealers charge less, but probably have sicker cars. They give warranties, but usually weaker ones than new car dealers give. Some give a "50–50" warranty. This means they pay half the repair cost. This sounds like a good deal but often it just means they pad the repair bill so you get stuck with the full repair cost anyway.

A private sale is where you probably will get the best price. Buy through the classified ads and you eliminate the middleman. There are problems, however. Harry, at the local bar, who gives you a great price on his old Chevy "because I've got to raise money for my divorce," may really be the head salesman for a stolen-car ring. Or maybe he's selling you the car because he hasn't made payments on it for two months and it's about to be repossessed. To check for theft, be sure the name printed on the title document is also the name of the person who's trying to sell you the car. Also, the VIN (Vehicle Identification Number) on the title should match the VIN number on the car. (It's printed either on the engine, or dashboard or door.) No match? Might be stolen.

The title also tells you if the seller still owes money on the car. Look for First National Bank or Household Finance or whatever on the corner or back of the title. If he owns the car free and clear, he would have received a new title, without the finance company's name on it. Or, if he doesn't have the new title yet, he should have some note from the finance company to prove he paid the loan. If he says he's using the sale money (your money) to pay off the loan, I suggest you go with him to the finance company and let them organize the paperwork.

Finance companies hire detective agencies to repossess cars

for them. (What a job these guys have! They creep around until they find cars on their repossess list, then jump out, break into the car, hot-wire it, and drive off as quickly as they can, terrified that the furious owner is about to run out with a shotgun. It takes them two minutes to "steal" the car.) If the car you just bought has already been put on the detective agency's repossess list, they won't know that you are a new owner; they'll just "steal" the car. You then call the police to report the theft. The police say, "Oh, that car was repossessed, not stolen" (the detective agency reports its repossessions to the police). You call the detective agency. The detective agency refers you to the finance company. The finance company, after 3,418¼ phone calls back and forth, tells the detective agency to give you the car back. You get the car back, three weeks later, with a broken lock and ignition. It's easier to let the finance company reorganize the paperwork *before* you buy.

To be extra safe, call the Motor Vehicles Department (under state government listings in the phone book). You have to call the MVD anyway to register the car. Ask them if the title's numbers and names match those on their copy of the title. This protects you if a stolen-car seller has come up with a phony title certificate.

The stolen-car problem is not confined to private sales. Nancy Zucker, of Long Island, New York, bought a used BMW from a new car dealer for $11,000. (The following is an abridged transcript of a report on WCBS-TV News:)

Nancy Zucker: The dealer called me up and said, "The BMW is a stolen car. Bring it in." I said, "No, I'm not going to bring it in until you give me my money back." He said, "It doesn't work that way."

John Stossel: The police came and took the car away from her. That left her with no car . . . and from the dealer, no money back.

Nancy Zucker: The dealer's position is "Sue me!"

I eventually got the dealer to give Ms. Zucker a new car. It is his responsibility to make sure any car he sells has a clear-and-free title, and I could hold him to that. But that's because he was an established dealer. If you buy through the classifieds, you may have trouble even *finding* the seller once the police tow your car away.

One final disadvantage to private sales: the seller doesn't offer financing. I don't find this important, however, because the financing dealer's offer is generally lousy anyway (see page 14). *Another choice: Buy from Hertz or Avis.* Hertz and Avis rent new cars, so they sell the old ones. Most have about 25,000 miles on them. The younger ones carry twelve-month warranties, the older ones three months. Many of these cars are good buys.

You may think I'm crazy to recommend this. After all, people abuse rental cars—we drive them much more roughly than we'd ever drive our own cars. However, with our own cars we often ignore owner's manual instructions about oil changes, etc. Rental cars are at least regularly maintained, and maintenance can be more important than how a car is driven.

Hertz has been accused of misrepresenting the quality of their used cars by not telling customers about prior accidents. Hertz denies misrepresenting anything. To protect yourself, ask for the car's repair record. It tells you what injuries the car has suffered. Another advantage of buying from rental companies is that they all have repair records available; that's not true of other used car dealers.

RECALLS

Before you start driving any used car (or better yet, before you make the purchase), I suggest you call 800-424-9393 to find out if it was ever recalled. For all you know, the brakes may be about to fail. Inserting one small bolt (something a new car dealer will do for free, under the terms of the recall) would solve the problem *if* you knew to have it done. The previous owner probably was notified of the recall but ignored it (most car owners do not respond to recall notices—too much trouble, I guess). Give the people at 800-424-9393 (it's a government hotline) the year and make of your car, and they'll tell you if there's a recall out on it.

REPAIRS

Look, I'd really like to help you on this one, but I don't think I can. Not much, anyway. I could say what all the consumer advice books say: "Go only to a reputable garage." Great. Now tell me how you know which ones are reputable.

Fixing your car is like going to a doctor. We don't know what's going on in there, so we have to trust someone. If they want to cheat us, they will.

SOME TRICKS TO REDUCE THE DAMAGE:

Check with your local auto club to see if there's a diagnostic center in your area. For a flat fee, diagnostic clinics run electronic tests on your car and give you a readout indicating the problems. Diagnostic centers usually don't have their own repair shops, so they have no incentive to cheat you. If they do have a repair shop, make it clear that you plan to have the repairs done somewhere else.

Choose a garage that has a machine called an "engine analyzer." One U.S. Transportation Department study found most bad or unnecessary repairs are done not because the mechanic cheats, but because he is incompetent. The engine analyzer is better than most mechanics at figuring out what's wrong with your engine. Not all shops have the analyzers, but chances are at least one garage in your area will.

Watch the mechanic do the work. You may not know what he's doing, but *he* doesn't know that.

If you think you've been ripped off, call your state Motor Vehicles Department. In many states, Motor Vehicles departments will arbitrate between you and the dealer. They might get your money back. So might an AutoCAP office, if a dealer is the source of your repair problem. AutoCAP is a dealers' association. You might suspect they always take the dealer's side (they often do), but AutoCAP claims to resolve most complaints to the customer's satisfaction. To check if there is an AutoCAP office in your area, look in the phone book for your city's or county's Automobile Dealer's Association.

GETTING A LEMON

It's not fair. You've saved years for your dream car and now it leaks, creaks and breaks down so often, the repairman recognizes your ring when you call. Your car is still under warranty, but it won't be for much longer, and it's already cost you a fortune in cab fares and lost work time. You've asked the automaker for another car since yours is clearly irrepairable, but the automaker said, "No. All cars are repairable. I know you've been to the dealer ninety-five times, but I'm sure if you bring it back one more time, he'll be able to fix the problem."

I get more complaints about car lemons than anything else. Unfortunately, there's very little you can do about it. The automakers will not give you a new car. Their general policy: "If you don't like it, sue us." They can say that quite cockily because they know that the lawyer will probably cost you more than the car. It's too bad, because you might win a lawsuit. Ron Pavesi of Lakewood, New Jersey, did:

(The following is an abridged transcript of a report on WCBS-TV News.)

Stossel: You got the car, and what happened?

Pavesi: A day later I came back with the paint peeling off the front hood. I wanted a new car or my money back.

Stossel: Ford said they would not give you a new car, but they would paint it.

Pavesi: That's right.

Stossel: And, so they painted it.

Pavesi: That's right. And, about three weeks later, it peeled again.

Stossel: You asked for a new car.

Pavesi: That's right. I said I don't accept this car. I wanted my money back or a new car. Again, they told me they will repair the car, but under no circumstances will they give me a new car.

Stossel: So they repaired it.

Pavesi: That's right. About three weeks later it peeled again.

Stossel: Three times it happened.

Stossel: (to Paul Larson, Owner, Larson Ford): He came to you and said the paint's peeling, and he wanted a new car, but you wouldn't give it to him.

Larson: Well, because the normal policy at Ford Motor Company or any manufacturer is to repair the vehicle to its original condition.

Stossel: When it appeared that you couldn't repair the car, shouldn't he have gotten a new one?

Larson: Well, if every time a person had a complaint on a vehicle, they had to replace the car, why, it would sort of destroy the whole automotive industry.

Dubious reasoning, I think. No one is asking the automaker to replace every problem car, just the obvious lemons: the ones that need repair again and again and again. Ron Pavesi was lucky in that his lawyer got so mad about Ford's attitude that he took the case for nothing. They sued and won; a New Jersey court said Ford's "attitude was unconscionable" and ordered Ford to give Pavesi his money back.

Hurray for Pavesi, but it's not much help for us. Had his lawyer not worked for free, Pavesi would have paid maybe $6,000 in legal fees to replace a $5,000 car. If you sue and win, there's a chance the judge will order the automaker to pay your lawyer's fees. I wouldn't count on it, however; often you have to prove fraud to get legal fees, and to show fraud is tough. You may have to prove the automaker is ripping you off intentionally.

A better solution if you buy a lemon is to simply be obnoxious. Bob Kennedy of Greenwich, Connecticut, built "superlemon," a giant wooden lemon which he parked in front of the dealership that sold him the car. The dealer promptly gave him a new one. Other lemon owners have gotten their cars replaced by picketing the dealers. The point: The dealer may decide replacing the car is better than getting bad publicity. The risk is that the dealer may sue you for harassment or libel. If you make accusations (on a picket sign, for example) against your dealer (or any business), make sure you can prove the accusations are true.

The best cure for a lemon is prevention. Get the kinks out before you pay for the car (see page 14).

DEALING WITH WINTER

During the first cold snap, I usually go over to the American

Automobile Club's towing headquarters and tag along as they go out to rescue motorists who can't get their cars started. Amazingly, seldom do the AAA mechanics have to do anything mechanical to the car. Most often, the mechanic simply hops in the car and starts it. The driver stands there looking foolish and says something like, "I can't understand it . . . I tried it a dozen times and it just wouldn't start." Most often, the driver's mistake is pumping the gas pedal. That's how I was taught to start a car in cold weather, but pumping is dead wrong. The correct way: Depress the gas pedal *once* (that sets the choke). Let the pedal all the way up. Then turn the key.

If you have been pumping the gas pedal, you probably flooded the car. The way to get it unflooded is to press the pedal all the way down, hold it there, then turn the key and keep the ignition on until the car turns over. Remember, the battery loses much of its power in cold weather, so make sure the lights, radio, heater, etc., are off before you try to start the car. This seems obvious, but one in four times the tow truck is called, the driver was trying to start the car with at least one of the battery-drainers on.

Frozen gas lines are another reason cars don't start. Gas doesn't freeze easily, but water does, so if there's water mixed with your gas, you're in trouble in cold weather. You're most likely to get water in the gas if you've been driving with very little gas in the tank. The less gas, the more air there is in the tank; as air gets cold, water condenses out of it. The simple solution: Keep the tank nearly full most of the winter.

The AAA also suggests you carry the following items in your car during the winter:

1. A shovel for digging out.
2. Sand to put under the wheels for traction. Put it in a closed container because if it gets wet, it freezes as hard as a rock.
3. A piece of screen (also to put under the tire for traction).
4. De-icer. Not just for removing ice from the windshield, but also for thawing frozen locks (just spray into the keyhole). Heating the key with a match also helps thaw the lock.

In a cold climate, you of course need to add antifreeze to your radiator. Anti*freeze* is a somewhat misleading term; more accurate would be antifreeze/antiboil because antifreeze not only lowers the freezing point of water, it also raises the boiling point. Antifreeze, therefore, also helps keep your car from overheating in the summer. This is especially important with air-conditioned cars, because cooling the inside of the car adds extra heat to the engine.

Antifreeze makers suggest you change antifreeze once a year. Of course, they're trying to sell more of their product. You, however, can get away with changing only every two years, if you have no radiator problems. Some people think you can tell when the old stuff is no longer working by how cloudy it is. Bull, say the experts: have a service station test it. If you put it in yourself, remember to dilute it; for every quart of antifreeze, add one quart of water. Adding pure antifreeze does your car no good and costs you twice as much.

I don't think the brand matters much. All brands use the same chemical, Ethylene Glycol, as a coolant. You might as well buy the cheapest.

One last idea: Run the air-conditioner once in a while during the winter. It keeps the seals from drying out.

RUST

Cars seem to rust faster these days. It's not that the metal is any different; it's because air pollution is worse, and cities use more salt to clear roads of ice and snow. Salt and pollution both eat through paint and help rust develop.

The time to stop rust is before it starts. Ford recommends repainting nicks and scratches immediately, washing your car once a week, and waxing it twice a year. When you wash the car, remember to spray up into the wheel housing (covers) to get rid of salt accumulation there. After the wash, dry the car by driving it. Standing wet in the garage encourages rust formation. Some experts suggest (the automakers aren't wild about this idea) that before you take delivery of a new car, take it to a car wash (remember you should test the new car before paying, anyway . . . see page 14). After the wash, if you find water in the trunk, or on the floor pads, or if the windows leak, you should take it back to the dealer and demand the leaks be fixed. No fix, no pay; new cars should be watertight.

You can also go to a rust-proofer. They'll coat your car with extra sealant for about $150; some will guarantee the rust-proofing. Car dealers will also offer rust-proofing, but *Road and Track* says they're generally less efficient than independent rust-proofers.

Is it worth the $150? It depends on how you use your car. If you keep it in a garage, wash and wax it regularly, don't drive in snowy areas or near oceans (salt from the spray), you probably don't need rust-proofing.

GETTING BETTER MILEAGE

You know the obvious stuff: avoid jackrabbit starts, take the weight out of the car (remove the books you store in the trunk), keep the engine tuned, etc.

Less obvious:

QUESTION: On a hilly terrain, you use less gas if you:
   a. Keep your foot steady on the pedal.
   b. Accelerate at the start of the hill.
   c. Accelerate before the start of the hill.

The answer is C. Early acceleration gives you momentum going into the hill and therefore you burn less gas.

QUESTION: On a hot day, at 55 mph, you use less gas:
   a. Running the air-conditioner.
   b. Opening the windows and putting the car on "vent."

The answer, surprisingly, is A. Opening the windows interferes with the car's aerodynamics, so that running the air-conditioner is actually cheaper.

Note: This applies only at highway speeds; if you're driving more slowly, you save by opening windows. Also, older, pre-1977 cars have such inefficient air-conditioners that running the air-conditioner always burns extra gas.

QUESTION: On a cold day, before driving off, let your car warm up by idling for:

    a. 30 seconds.
    b. 2 minutes.
    c. 5 minutes.

The answer is *A*. Any more idling is waste. However, you should drive slowly until the engine is completely warmed up. Other tips:

1. Avoid idling. Starting and stopping the engine uses as much gas as idling 1 minute. So, if you plan to wait longer than a minute, it's cheaper to kill the engine. You can drive a mile on the gas it takes to idle the car for 2 minutes.

2. Most of us seldom check tire pressure. If the pressure is low, your car burns 5% more gas.

3. Buy lower octane. Putting a higher octane gas in your car does *nothing* for it. You won't get better mileage; the car won't perform better. You are just wasting money. Your owner's manual will tell you what octane you should use. It might even be right. A better method, however, is trial and error, because even identical model cars have differing tastes in fuel. The trick: Try a lower octane gas (octane levels are posted on the pump). If the car runs okay, try a still lower octane. If the car knocks (I asked mechanics to describe the knocking sound. Most could not. Some said, "It's like a 'ping.'" One said, "It's like falling in love; you'll know it when it's happening"), go back to the higher octane. Don't worry, one tankful of mild knocking won't damage your car. Your ideal octane may vary from gas station to gas station (some stations lie) and place to place (altitude can change octane requirements). Be flexible.

GAS-SAVING DEVICES

What about those wonderful products advertised in the papers? "Add Slimeze to your tank! Get better mileage." Numerous organizations have run tests on these devices. To my knowledge the only one that ever passed is a device called "Pass-

Saver." It cuts off the air-conditioning when you accelerate. Pass-Saver will probably pay for itself if you live in a climate where you use air-conditioning most of the time.

Most other devices are a waste of money, even those put out by respectable companies. Union Carbide, for example, manufactures "Gas Miser." Pour it down the tank and it promises to give you "an extra ten miles per tankful." If true, that's great. Or at least it *sounds* great until you compute it. Assuming you get 20 miles per gallon, 10 extra miles means you save one-half gallon per tankful; in other words, maybe 75¢. Gas Miser costs $1.29. So you come out 54¢ behind. Union Carbide, thanks a lot.

DIESEL CARS

The advertising promises: "More miles per gallon! Fuel is easier to get!" Diesel *may be* a prudent alternative; at times during gas shortages diesel was much easier to get than regular gas. But:

There's no guarantee that diesel will continue to be more available than regular gas. If there's a serious shortage, diesel sales might be restricted to trucks only. Diesel has been slightly cheaper than regular gas, but there's no guarantee it will continue to be.

Aside from that, diesel's *advantages:*

Better mileage.

Less maintenance. There's no carburetor, no spark plugs or points, so you need fewer tune-ups.

Disadvantages:

Noise. The engine simply makes more noise. This doesn't bother me, or most diesel owners. The noise is louder outside the car than in.

Smell. There is a temporary stink of diesel fuel when you start the car.

Acceleration. Diesel cars have less pickup than ordinary cars.

Fewer gas stations. Diesel manufacturers provide guidebooks that tell you the location of diesel gas stations. These stations, however, are often few and far between, and they're often closed at night. Once when test driving a diesel, I just could not find an open diesel station. It was midnight. I was far from home. I spent the night sleeping in the back seat. No fun. On the other hand, since diesel fuel is the same as home heating oil, I could have sneaked into someone's backyard, and siphoned it out of their home tank. That didn't seem very safe, but in an emergency. . . ?

LEASING

If you buy a new car every two years or so, consider leasing instead of buying. Leasing can be cheaper, depending on the deal you get, but it usually isn't. To figure the costs, you total the down payment, the interest . . . (Frankly, figuring this out is so complicated and boring that I don't want to bother with it. If you really want to do the calculations, get the April, 1979 issue of *Consumer Reports;* it contains a leasing guide. In any case, leasing is not going to save or cost you more than a few dollars.) The point: If you hate the hassle of buying and reselling a car, then lease. If you use your car for business and need regular invoices for tax deductions, leasing might help. Let your accountant be your guide.

Otherwise, buy. It's *usually* cheaper.

SAFETY

I do scary reports on television about the dangers of eating bacon, working with asbestos, flying in small planes, etc., yet the chance we'll die from doing those things is minute compared to the chance we'll die driving in a car.

Wearing seat belts really does save lives. *Most* people who die in accidents would not have died had they been wearing belts. After years of watching slow-motion car crashes (as the film editor pulls the film back and forth through the viewer), I *always* wear seat belts.

When more cars come out with airbags as options I'll buy one of them too. I've had the bags explode in my face. It's not that scary. Car crashes scare me much more.

PROTECTING YOUR CHILD

The design of cars is most dangerous for children. Yes, there's a padded dashboard, but the small child misses the padding and hits the hard part underneath. Studies show child-safety seats could save the lives of 9 out of 10 children killed in crashes, yet most parents don't use them. Holding a child in your arms doesn't help; the force of the crash breaks your hold, and even if it didn't, your own weight can crush the youngster.

Not all child-safety seats are equally good. Here's a list of those recommended by Michigan's Office of Safety Planning: Michigan suggests infants be put only in seats that face the rear of the car. Children old enough to sit up on their own (Michigan calls them "Toddlers") may face forward.

BRAND	MANUFACTURER
Recommended for infants only	
Dyn-o-Mite	Questor
Infant Love Seat	General Motors-Chrysler-Ford
Trav-L-Ette	Century

Recommended for toddlers and infants (These seats are convertible; they may be used facing front or rear).

Bobby Mac Two-in-One #810	Bobby Mac Co.
Bobby Mac Deluxe #812	Bobby Mac Co.
Bobby Mac Super Car Seat #987, #814	Bobby Mac Co.
Kantwet Car Seat #987, #988	Questor
Peterson Safety Shell	Cosco
Peterson Safe-T-Seat #78	Cosco
Safe-N'Easy #13-203	Cosco
Safe-N'Easy Recliner #13-313	Cosco
Trav-L-Guard	Century
Strolee We Care Car Seat #597S	Strolee

(Not recommended for infants in rear-facing position.)

Recommended for toddlers

GM Child Love Seat	General Motors
Kantwet Fitz-All Deluxe #597	Questor
Mopar Child Shield	Chrysler
Toddler Car Seat #595	Strolee
Tot Guard	Ford

Buy one. It's a good investment. Buy one of the seats that's on the list. Michigan found many safety seats did *not* provide much protection.

TIRES

BUYING THEM

At last, after years of quarreling with the industry, the government has come up with a tire-rating system. Now you can find out that $30 tires would have been just as good as the $45 tires you just bought.

The ratings are printed on the tire sidewall. Sample: Treadwear 150, Traction A, Temperature C. Here's how it works:

Treadwear: The higher the number, the longer a tire should last. The government tests treadwear on a Texas test course. If a tire lasts 30,000 miles on this course, it gets a 100 rating, a 150-rated tire should last 50% longer, or 45,000 miles.

Traction: This is a test of a tire's ability to stop, particularly on wet pavement. A is the best traction, C the worst.

Temperature: In this test, tires are run at high speeds in a hot room. Tires that overheat and fall apart first get a C rating, those that resist the heat best are rated A. If you do only stop-and-go city driving, you could probably get away with a C temperature tire. If you do a lot of summer highway driving, an A is a must. Caution: if a tire is low on air, it gets even hotter than normal.

TAKING CARE OF TIRES

Underinflating tires is the most common maintenance mistake. The U.S. Transportation Department did a spot check and found half the tires it examined underinflated.

An underinflated tire is dangerous (more likely to overheat and blowout) and wasteful (they don't roll so well; the car uses more gas).

Overinflated tires are no bargain either. They give you a rougher ride and are more susceptible to cuts and bruises from debris on the road. Correct tire pressure is listed on a sticker attached to your car's doorpost or glove compartment. Service-station pressure testers are often inaccurate, so don't always go to the same station to have the pressure checked. Temperature affects pressure, so don't check the tires immediately after a long drive. The heat buildup will give you an abnormally high reading. Let the tires cool before you test. Also, cold weather reduces tire pressure (remember high school physics? . . . the molecules move closer together in the cold) so you may need to add air at the beginning of winter, and let some out in the spring.

WORRYING ABOUT TIRES

The less tread on the tire, the less traction you get. Bald tires are particularly dangerous on wet roads. Since there are no grooves into which the water can escape, the rubber just pushes the water along, creating an effect much like driving a sled in the snow.

How much tread is too little? Stick a penny in the groove. If you can still see all of Lincoln's head, that's too little tread. If some of your tires are better than others, put the good ones on the rear wheels; rear tires are more important for good traction on curves.

If you're mixing types of tires, mix them front to back, not side to side. In other words, don't put a radial on the left and a belted-bias on the right. It would be like trying to run wearing one sneaker and one roller skate. If you have only two radials, put them on the rear. Radials on the front alone make the car harder to handle.

If any tire wears unevenly, see a mechanic. Uneven wear is often a sign that your car is misaligned.

IN THE SNOW

Radials are no substitute for snow tires, according to the Tire Industry Safety Council. Yes, radials are a little better than ordinary tires, but in snow, the deep grooves of a snow tire grab at the snow and give much better traction. On ice, snow tires give you slightly better traction because the rubber is a little softer. They also wear out sooner, so it pays to put your regular tires back on immediately after the snow season ends. If you have a front-wheel-drive car, remember to put the snow tires on the front (they go on whichever axle is propelling the car). Four-wheel drive cars need four snow tires.

Rotating tires may make then last longer. I suggest you do it when putting on the snow tires. When you put the snow tires on the rear axle, move the rear tires to the front, and store the front tires. (Be careful to store them flat; don't balance them on the edge of the tread or the tire will warp. If the tires are off the rims, don't hang them up.) At winter's end, when you put the stored tires on the rear axle, you'll have your best (least used) tires in the rear, where they belong.

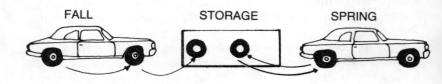

FALL   STORAGE   SPRING

INSURANCE

The less the better, with one exception: liability coverage.

Liability covers you if someone sues you because you injured them. These suits can cost hundreds of thousands of dollars. I suggest $300,000 liability coverage. It costs only a few dollars more than $100,000 protection.

Your insurance company will also try to sell you collision and comprehensive insurance. You may have to buy both if your car is being financed, but if it's not required, I'd think twice about buying either. Here's why: Collision insurance covers the cost of repairing your car after an accident. As the insurance company knows, the odds are that you won't have an accident, and even if you do, you'll probably pay more in insurance premiums over your lifetime than you'll ever collect in reimbursements. The average cost of repairing the unlikely accident on a 1979 car is approximately $1,000. If you can afford to pay for the repairs yourself, you'll be richer in the long run buying no collision insurance.

The same is true of comprehensive coverage, which pays if your car is stolen, or damaged by flood, fire, vandalism, etc. Premiums are high. The odds say no insurance is best. This is big-time gambling, however; if you lose the bet (say the car is stolen), you're out the price of the car.

If you do buy comprehensive or collision insurance, at least get the highest deductible they offer. A $200 deductible means if the repair costs $1,000, the insurance company pays only $800; you pay $200. If the repair is less than $200, you pay it, the insurance company never hears about it, and they don't raise your premium to punish you for being a reckless driver. You also get to deduct the $200 repair at tax time. The higher the deductible, the lower the premium (see following chart). If you get a high deductible, not only are you likely (according to accident statistics) to pay less in the long run, but you are also less likely to have to suffer through your insurance company's accident paperwork. More money, less arguing.

HOW DEDUCTIBLE AFFECTS PREMIUM

COLLISION INSURANCE *

Deductible	Premium
$100	$402/year
$200	$335
$300	$285
$500	$218

COMPREHENSIVE INSURANCE *

Deductible	Premium
$ 50	$204/year
$100	$162
$200	$141
$300	$128
$500	$113

* Statistics apply to 1980 Chevy Impala in Manhattan, married driver, over 25, good driving record.

When price-shopping for insurance, be aware that some, although not all, companies offer discounts for: (1) good driving records; (2) two-car families; (3) nonsmokers; (4) nondrinkers; (5) graduates of driver-education courses; (6) students with good grades; (7) owners of cars with lower than average repair-cost records.

If your company doesn't offer the discounts that apply to you, try some other companies. You might save hundreds of dollars in premiums.

Buying a House

It's amazing how careless people are about buying a house. People who clip coupons to save 12¢ on a can of peas will buy a $75,000 house after visiting only three and spending less than an hour inspecting each. This amazes realtors too, but they don't care. The fewer houses you visit, the less time you spend deciding, the better for them. Experts suggest you visit twenty houses before you buy. Why not? This is by far the biggest purchase you're ever likely to make. Looking at different houses is fun, anyway.

First decision: How much can you afford? Financial experts say your monthly house payment should be no more than one week's salary (before deductions). If the payments are higher you may have trouble meeting them, and you could lose the house to the bank. Your bank or a real estate agent will tell you approximate monthly payments on differently priced houses. For example, a $100,000 house would cost you $702 a month if you get a 10% 30-year mortgage (this assumes you put 20% or $20,000 down, so you are getting an $80,000 loan). Add perhaps $300 for taxes and insurance, and it means you should be making at least $702 + $300 = $1002 a week to *comfortably* afford the monthly payment.

Once you've determined the price and the features (number of bedrooms, etc.) you want, go to a real estate broker/agent in the area you would like to live.

The agent will ask you what you want in a house and how much you can pay, then tell you there's no way you can get what you've described for your price and you'll just have to settle for less. Perhaps the agent will drive you to houses that meet all your specifications, but then shock you with the cost. Why we have unrealistic expectations about house values is a mystery to me, but almost everyone does. Take heart. Others who were first disappointed found livable houses. You can always make improvements later, when you have more money.

That brings us to another point: you can always improve the house, but you're stuck with the neighborhood. Neighborhood should be a prime concern in picking a place to live. A mildly improved house in a good neighborhood will have more resale value than a much improved house in a crummy neighborhood.

THE REAL ESTATE AGENT

Agents can be a great help in finding a house, and a good source of information about local taxes, transportation, schools, neighborhood characteristics, etc. After all, the agent usually lives in the neighborhood being shown. But don't expect *too* much.

The agent makes money only when the house is sold, and is not about to mention hidden disadvantages. If there is a smelly garbage dump a few blocks to the north, the agent may show you that house only when the wind is blowing from the south. The agent probably won't tell you about hidden structural problems, and probably wouldn't recognize them anyway. A realtor is primarily a sales agent, not a housing expert. Also, the agent usually has no interest in helping you persuade the seller to lower the price. The higher the price, the bigger the agent's commission. Of course, if the only way to get a sale is if the price comes down a bit, the agent will help you bargain. House prices are almost always negotiable; and the longer a house has been on the market, the less you should offer for it, because the owner is usually more hungry to sell.

Most real estate brokers operate under a multiple listing system. This means when a seller calls a broker and says, "I want to sell my house," all brokers are notified of the availability. Because of this system, agents tell you there's no point in a buyer contacting more than one agent, "After all, we all have the same listings." Bunk. A broker who gets a listing isn't eager to let competing brokers get wind of it. At least not right away. A few days' delay may be enough time for one of the agents to make the sale. Why not? Why give away a fat commission? This is particularly true of houses the broker thinks will sell quickly; and these houses are of course the best buys. When I shopped for my house I found that by going to several brokers, I received numerous exclusive listings from each; yet all these businesses were supposedly participating in the "multiple listing" system. If you have time, try several agents. And why not take them out to dinner, make friends? Maybe then you'll be the first they call when a great new house comes on the market. This is big business; thousands of dollars are at stake; why not do some wining and dining? Colleges do it to get high school football players—you might as well do it to get a house.

EXAMINING THE HOUSE

Enough scheming. Back to the practical. When the agent is showing you the house, take notes. Most people don't. Most of us rely on memory. This is ridiculous. How can we possibly remember all the details of several houses, much less evaluate them under the pressure of a sales pitch? If you write things down, you'll be able to make comparisons at your leisure when you get home. It's also a good idea to bring a tape measure, so you can make accurate comparisons of stuff like hallway widths and closet space.

Assuming the termites don't greet you at the door, you probably won't see any structural defects. The seller, not being an idiot, has probably had obvious defects repaired or hidden (is there fresh paint, a picture in an odd place? Maybe it's hiding a crack). I think the best move is to hire a professional home inspector. Look under "Home Inspection" or "Building Inspection" in the Yellow Pages; or safer, ask your mortgage banker to recommend someone. Home inspectors charge about $150 (piddly stuff compared to the price of a house). They are usually architects, or builders, or engineers, and they will spend an hour or two poking around the house looking for problems. Not only will the inspector tell you what these defects are, but also what they would cost to fix.

A house with problems may still be worth buying, if the price is low and the repairs cheap. If you decide there are too many defects for the price, you can use the home inspector's report to negotiate a lower price for the house. Once you tell the seller, "Hey, I've got this list here which shows all these defects, . . ." the seller may be willing to lower the asking price.

Inspectors rip people off too. Some exaggerate a house's flaws to justify their fee. Beware of inspectors who offer to make the repairs themselves. They may have exaggerated defects in order to profit by repairing them. Nevertheless, most realtors suggest hiring an inspector and there are a number, listed in every town, who are not in the repair business.

In addition, there are several tests you can do on your own: go to the basement and look for stains or discolorations on the walls or floor, particularly where they join. These are warnings of water problems. A basement that is dry in summer may be swimmable by spring. If you're shopping in cold weather, test the insulation by standing in the corners of several rooms, putting one hand on a wall that faces outdoors, the other hand on an interior wall. If the interior wall is noticeably warmer, there's not enough insulation. Better yet, ask to see the owner's heating bills. Look at the bills yourself; don't just ask; sellers lie like crazy. Plumbing repairs are very expensive, so check the water pressure (run the shower).

Structural damage is the most expensive repair. If the house you buy is settling, it could cost you a fortune. One test is to open and close some of the windows. If the house is settling, many of the windows will probably be stuck shut. Termites are another expensive problem. For tips on finding them, see page 51. The seller will probably lie about the age of a house unless it is old enough for its age to be an asset. To double-check, lift the lid off the toilet tanks. The date stamped on the bottom of the lid is the date the toilet was made. Although some houses have new toilets, I don't think many new houses have used toilets, so you can assume the house is *at least* as old as the date on the lid. If you can't find the date, don't go crazy searching; it's not printed on *all* toilets.

NEW HOUSES VS. OLD HOUSES

New houses usually have better plumbing, wiring, and insulation.

Older houses usually have bigger rooms and more complete landscaping.

BUILDING A NEW HOUSE

There are plenty of horror stories. Sometimes you fall in love with the model house, put $10,000 down, and the builder goes to Brazil with your money. Sometimes he builds the house but does such a lousy job that it is already falling apart when you move in. Sometimes he assures you it will be completed by May, but it's not ready until July. Actually . . . I think that always happens. Something else that almost always happens is that as the house is going up, you see all kinds of things you'd like changed. The builder happily changes these things and collects a fat profit on each modification. Expect the house to cost more than you planned. The amount depends on the number of changes, but 10% is not uncommon.

Paying 10% more is better than getting no house. No house is what some people in Staten Island, New York, got:

(The following is an abridged transcript of a report on WCBS-TV News:)

Stossel: "How much deposit did you give them?"

Annette Leonard: "All told—$4,300. . . ."

Stossel: "$4,300. And this empty lot is your house?"

Annette Leonard: "Yes—isn't it beautiful?"

Stossel: "And it's supposed to be done when?"

Annette Leonard: "Well, it said November 1st on the contract. . . ."

Stossel: November 1st was more than six months ago. Now it looks as if the house will never be finished. The bank says the builder, Thomaso Ravesoneri, seems to have just run out of money and walked away from the project. The Leonards will probably not get their money back.

Annette Leonard: "I think it's disgusting. I mean I'm not the only one. I think there are a lot of people and a lot of money involved in this."

Stossel: That's for sure. There are, for example, the people whose homes were started, but not finished. One house just collapsed. Others are still standing, but they've been vandalized. I doubt that anyone will be able to live in them. Some houses were nearly finished, and so when the contractor stopped work, people just moved in. The mortgage bank allowed them to stay as squatters. What are your rights in a situation like this? If the builder does not fulfill his end of the contract, you have the right to sue him for damages, breach of contract. But in this case, what's the point of hiring a lawyer? Even if you won the suit, if the construction company is out of money, there would be no money for you to win. A builder is not required to post a bond, nor does he have to put your deposit in escrow. For all I know, he could have spent your money on champagne.

Barry Corn: "It took us a long time to save this money, and I just can't see how any one man could come by and take $4,000 from 22 people—that's $88,000—and do nothing but this."

Stossel: I couldn't find Ravesoneri, the builder, at his office or anywhere else. Neither can the home buyers.

Barry Corn: "His office is closed down. His phone is unlisted."

Stossel: "What happens when you try to call the attorney for the builder?"

Barry Corn: "Well, you get his—er—the secretary, I guess. And she tells you: 'He's not here right now. I'll take a message.' That's the end of it. You never—you never hear another word. You cannot get in touch with the man."

Stossel: I tried. I walked into his office, cameras rolling. He wasn't in. "Do you think we should wait?"

Woman in attorney's office: "No, I don't advise you to wait."

Stossel: "Er—alright. Would he call me up if I leave my number?"

Woman in attorney's office: "Yes."

Stossel: He never did.

There's no foolproof way to protect yourself, but here are three simple precautions:

1. Call the builder's bank. Ask about his financial standing. If

they won't tell *you,* they might tell your bank. Have your mortgage banker make the call.

2. Visit the builder's last development. Walk around, knock on doors. Ask people if they are happy with their houses. Don't be shy about it; people *love* to talk about their homes. They'll probably tell you they wish they had done what you are doing. You may get ideas for features you'd like in your house.

3. Withhold some money. Try to work a clause into the contract that says the last $5,000 or so is held in escrow until *everything* is done. When you control the money, the builder has an incentive to do the work.

A good lawyer will suggest other ways to protect you. Unfortunately, a lawyer costs a fortune; generally up to 1% of the value of the house. Some people save money by not hiring lawyers. Lawyers, of course, say that's risky. To find a good real estate lawyer, ask your mortage bank for a recommendation. Ask them "which lawyers' closings go smoothly?"

A builder may offer a warranty on his houses. It could be a crackpot warranty, because if the builder is a crook, or runs into financial trouble, he's not going to be around to back it up. If the warranty is a H.O.W. warranty, however, you are in better shape. H.O.W. is a warranty sponsored by the National Association of Home Builders. They get a bunch of reputable builders together and pool their money into a fund that helps pay for any defects. The warranty gives you free repairs on most defects for two years, and on major defects for up to ten years. If your builder disappears, the other builders pay for your repairs. Warning: Some crooked builders are not above offering H.O.W. warranties when they are in fact not H.O.W. members. You can check by writing H.O.W. at The National Association of Home Builders, 15th and M streets, N.W., Washington, D.C. 20005 Phone: 202-452-0200.

GETTING THE MORTGAGE

Your real estate agent will recommend places where you might get a mortgage. I suggest you try your own bank first;

many banks give preferential treatment to depositors who've had accounts for six months (sometimes one year). But don't stop there. It's vital to shop around for the mortgage. Three phone calls could save you $12,000: one bank in your neighborhood may be charging 10%, another 10½%, another 11%. Even a ½% difference on a $50,000 30-year mortgage will cost you $6,300 over the life of the loan! Shopping around is easy. Simply call the bank. Ask for the mortgage department. Tell them the price and location of the house you want to buy, and ask if you would be eligible for a mortgage. Then ask the interest rate. Many banks will tell you you're not eligible becuase you are not a depositor, but you might as well try. As I said, the savings on just a ½% difference will be enough to pay a kid to cut your lawn for the next sixty years.

Savings banks generally offer cheaper rates than commercial banks, though the former sometimes charge "points" on a mortgage. The "points" formula is a little confusing. Basically it means 1% extra is added, but only for the first year. So a 9% mortgage "with 2 points" is about equal to an 11% mortgage that turns into a 9% mortgage after one year.

SELLING YOUR HOUSE

The easiest way is to call a realtor and say, "I want to sell my house." They'll come over and tell you what they think it's worth, and place it on the multiple listings. Their opinion on what you can get for your home is usually an accurate one. They know what's realistic. They also have little incentive to quote a low price, because the more you get, the more they get. To be extra safe, call several realtors.

Selling your house through a real estate broker does have one big disadvantage. You pay a whopping commission. Most realtors charge 6%, and some now charge 7 or 8%. The commission is subtracted from the selling price. On a $100,000 house, you can lose a fat $6,000 to the broker. You *keep* the $6,000 by selling the house yourself, without the broker. It's a pain, but it's possible.

Realtors have a vicious lobby. Whenever I've done a story about selling-a-house-yourself on TV, they write nasty letters and call my bosses to try to get me fired. Some even call me and say, "How can you suggest such a thing—look what it would do to us!" Well, I think somebody making up to $16,000 for one sale, just because they are lucky enough to have as their product a $200,000 house in an 8% commission neighborhood, is getting an awfully good deal.

You can bargain with the brokers, and perhaps lower their commissions to, say, 3 or 4%, but they won't try as hard to sell your house, since they have other houses for sale where they'll get a bigger cut.

If you want to try to sell your house yourself, without the middleman, here's how:

First find out what your house is worth. The best way is to learn what other houses in the neighborhood sold for, and compare your house to those. Then stick a FOR SALE BY OWNER sign on your lawn, run an ad in the Classifieds, and sit home to wait for the calls.

There are advantages and disadvantages to avoiding a broker as was discussed in the following report:

(The following is an abridged transcript of a report that appeared on WCBS-TV News:)

Stossel: Rabbi Dick Schachet and his wife, Jan, are trying to sell their thirteen-room, $70,000 house without a real estate broker.

Rabbi Dick Schachet, West Midwood, Brooklyn: "We have sold three homes, none of which went through brokers, so we were able to save broker's fees."

Stossel: "Why not go to a broker?"

Rabbi Dick Schachet: "Dollars and cents—strictly a matter of dollars and cents."

Stossel: "How much more do you think you can get for the house by selling it yourself?"

Rabbi Dick Schachet: "Around $4,000 more."

Stossel: "The commission would be $4,000?"

Rabbi Dick Schachet: "That's correct."

There are disadvantages to selling without a realtor:

Jan Schachet: ". . . People come in who I don't think are as serious as if they had gone to a broker first."

Stossel: "Sometimes people call you and then don't show up."

Jan Schachet: "Yeah."

Stossel: "How often does that happen?"

Rabbi Dick Schachet: "Oh, I would say about 25 percent of the time."

Jan Schachet: "They'll call and say—you know—they'd like to come over and see the house."

Stossel: "So you come home and wait for them to come."

Jan Schachet: "Yeah—and they don't come."

Rabbi Dick Schachet: "A disadvantage too is that we really have to be home every weekend to show the house to people. It ties us up completely."

Stossel: "Real estate brokers say it's foolish to do what you're doing."

Rabbi Dick Schachet: "I don't see why. If saving $2,000 or $4,000 is foolish, then maybe it is foolish. But I don't think it's foolish at all."

One other disadvantage: You can be fooled about what your house is worth. You might sell too cheaply, or price it too high and get no offers. You can ask neighbors what they paid for their houses, but that's not always reliable information. People exaggerate. Buyers tend to brag down; they want you to think they got a good deal. Sellers brag up; they want you to think the house is worth more than it really is. You can get the accurate figure by going to the county clerk's office; the sales transactions are recorded there. Or you can hire a professional appraiser. Look under "Real Estate Appraisers" in the Yellow Pages. Better yet, ask a bank for a recommendation. The appraisal will cost about $150 for an $80,000 home.

HOME IMPROVEMENTS

The rule of thumb is that for every dollar you spend, you get back about half when you resell the house. But some improvements pay off better than others.

What pays off: Most home buyers are dazzled by large, modern kitchens and bathrooms. Spend money creating those, and you may get all your investment back. Put in central air-conditioning or an energy-efficient wood-burning fireplace and you'll also get much of your money back. Simply adding square-footage, like an extra room, increases the house's value significantly, but *only* if the house is in a good neighborhood.

What doesn't pay off: Most outdoor improvements bring lesser returns. Add a swimming pool or a patio, and you will likely get less than half your investment back when you sell.

Play your cards right making improvements and you can get rich. Sam and Mary Weir became millionaires by pyramiding home improvements. Right after they married, they bought a dumpy house for $4,000 and started fixing it up.

(The following is an abridged transcript of a report on WCBS-TV News:)

Mary Weir: "It took us a year-and-a-half to do the first house. We could do that house in about six weeks now, because we know what we're doing."

Stossel: Eventually, they rented that house to someone else, and moved to another house that needed fixing. Soon, moving and fixing became a way of life. They went from house to house, each time making enough by renting or selling the old one to move to a better one. Eventually, Sam quit his job.

Sam Weir: "I was a chemist, and I guess after the fourth or fifth house I made some projections on how I was doing with the company and how we were doing in real estate. And I was obviously doing ten times better in real estate."

Stossel: Twelve years after they started, the Weirs have done twenty-six houses. They rent almost half. Others they've sold—usually for twice their purchase price. They paid $100,000 for the estate they're in now. If they sell, they expect to get four times that.

Mary Weir: "We have found that a house that needs a new heating system, new kitchens, and new bathrooms have prices that are incredibly depressed. The majority of the houses that we have bought we have not paid much more for than what the land was worth. And by bringing them back, that's where we've made the majority of the money."

Stossel: The Weirs' first rule is to pay for the neighborhood, not the house.

Sam Weir: "Because when you're done you have a good house in a good area. If you buy a good house in a bad area, you know, there's nowhere to go."

Stossel: Rule number two—don't try to make an old house look new. Instead, make use of old fixtures—like moldings. And know what kinds of improvements attract buyers. Take kitchens—old houses have them in the back near the servant's quarters. Today people want them in the center of the house.

Stossel: It all sounds easy, but it wasn't at first.

Mary Weir: "Walking through that door the first day with your few belongings—it's scary."

Stossel: If you plan to do something like that, the Weirs advise you to start with a two-family house. That way you can rent out the part that you've done and get some income while still working on the part in which you're living.

Unfortunately, some people who undertake improvements end up losing money. There are more ripoff artists in this field than most. Some are professional con men who move from city to city, contracting to do work, collecting advance payments, and then disappearing. Watch for a telltale come-on: "Hi, I've been doing some work in your neighborhood and I've got some extra concrete (or shingles) left over. I see you need some work on your driveway (or roof) and since I've got all the materials nearby, I'll give you a special discount. . . ."

The only way to protect yourself is to ask for references and then make *several* calls to those references. If you're like most people, you are reluctant to do this. It feels awkward and it may seem like you're calling the guy a liar. But if he does good work, he'll be proud to give references and will respect you for being a smart consumer. Calling the people may seem difficult, but remember, people love to be "experts." By asking them for advice, you give them a chance to show off and tell what they know. I call three references before I pay anyone to do work on my house. Calling the Better Business Bureau is another good precaution. They even have a list of names the traveling phonies frequently use: Carroll, Clark, Black, Halliday, Holden, Horne, Johnston, Karrigan, Keith, Logan, McDonald, McGavin, McMillan, Reid, Scott, Stewart, Townsley, Watson, White,

Williams, Williamson, Woods. Families using these names generally operate out of newish pickup trucks with out-of-state license plates. They demand payment in cash.

SWIMMING POOLS

Here's a home improvement that probably won't pay for itself when you sell the house, but it will add some value. Also, think how much you'll save not driving the kids to the beach.

There are two types: above-ground and in-ground.

The above-ground pool is the simplest and cheapest. It's usually just a metal shell lined with vinyl. The metal can be steel, which rusts, or aluminum, which doesn't rust, but costs more. Cost can be as little as $300—for a tiny pool you may be able to bring home from the store yourself—or as much as $5,000 for a fancy job with redwood decks, filters, etc.

In-ground pools cost more, from $6,000 to $14,000, because somebody's got to dig a hole first. It will probably last longer, and it adds more to the value of your house. After the contractors dig the hole they build a pool frame. Sometimes the frame is wood, which they cover with a vinyl liner; sometimes it's a steel mesh, which they spray with concrete (not great for cold climates because the concrete tends to crack).

Some costs a dealer might not tell you about:

1. You need liability insurance to protect you in case a drunken guest swims into the side of the pool and hurts himself, or the pool breaks and floods your neighbor's house. Your homeowner's insurance might cover pools, but it probably doesn't.

2. All kinds of leaves, bugs, and funny-looking slimy stuff gather in the pool, so you'll need to buy water cleaning chemicals (and vacuums, if you want to get fancy). Figure almost an hour's work a day and $30 a month (more for bigger pools) during the summer.

3. A built-in pool will add value to your house, so your property taxes will probably go up.

You can get badly burned buying a pool. There are plenty of fly-by-night dealers. The worst of them have no showrooms (because they may need to leave town in a hurry), and sell by phone, mail, or door-to-door. Just because a big newspaper carries their ad doesn't mean they're legitimate. Most newspapers take ads from anybody who pays, without checking. A typical fly-by-night approach is to say, "I'll give you a pool for a special low price so I can use yours as a model in your area." Don't believe it. Others offer "a 10-year unconditional guarantee," which is easy to promise, because the guy is going to skip town long before then anyway. It's better to deal with someone who has a showroom, since a showroom owner is less likely to disappear.

Showroom dealers have their tricks too. The most common is the old "bait and switch" ploy. They run ads for super-cheap pools. Once you're in the showroom they say, "Here it is!" and show you some sleazy thing that looks like a bathtub; you don't want it, but you're "baited." Then they "switch" you up to a more expensive model. You could probably get that same model for less at a showroom that didn't "bait-and-switch."

Also, some dealers tend to build pools that leak. Talk to at least three people for whom the dealer has recently installed a pool. It's worth the trip to see these pools in person, since you'll probably get good ideas for your own pool. A reputable dealer will be happy to give you references.

You probably will want to heat the pool (unheated pools tend not to be used much). Heating so much water isn't cheap: Figure $800 to $1,000 a year for a medium sized (18' x 36') pool; more if you have electric heat. A better idea is solar heat. Heating your home with the sun doesn't usually pay (yet), because you'll have to build an expensive heat-storage unit (a pile of rocks or a tank of water to store the sun's heat when the sun isn't shining). But with a pool, you already have the necessary storage unit: the pool itself stores the heat. Solar heat works so well with pools that people who've bought systems for $3,000 tell me that they made that much back in fuel savings in two or three years. The heaters work so well their owners have to turn them off occasionally to keep the pool from getting too hot. There are sleazy solar contractors around, too, however, so I'd demand to talk to past customers before I'd pay anything. If you're looking for a solar contractor, Solar Industries, Monmouth Airport Industrial Park, Farmingdale, New Jersey 07727 (201-938-7000), and Fafco, 235 Constitution Drive, Menlo Park, California 94025 (415-321-3650), have good reputations. If one of their offices cannot do the work in your area, they'll recommend someone who will.

Solar collectors can be pretty ugly, and they take up a lot of room in your backyard (you can also put them on the roof). On the other hand, the system is a great conversation piece. You're doing something good for your energy-starved country by having that funny contraption in your backyard. I'm surprised there aren't laws forbidding new installations of gas, oil, or electric heaters on pools. After all: (1) heated pools are hardly a necessity, and (2) the more ecological solar heater works just as well, or better.

TERMITES

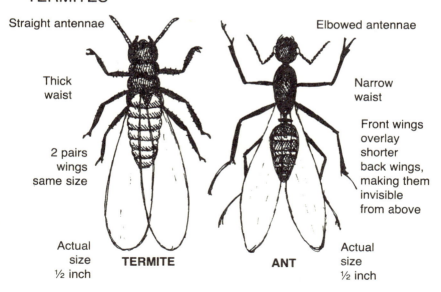

Straight antennae

Thick waist

2 pairs wings same size

Actual size ½ inch **TERMITE**

Elbowed antennae

Narrow waist

Front wings overlay shorter back wings, making them invisible from above

Actual size ½ inch

ANT

These nasty little bugs do little else with their lives but reproduce and eat. They eat cellulose, which makes them fond of newspapers, books and, unfortunately, the wood in your house. Spring is the time most people discover termites. When the sun warms the ground (or the walls of your house), termites get sexually aroused and start mating like crazy. This involves flying in a swarm; so if you see a swarm of what looks like flying ants in your basement this spring, call the exterminator. On the other hand, maybe they really are flying ants, so before panicking, compare them to the insects shown on page 51. You notice the termite has a larger waist than the flying ant. Eating houses apparently fattens them up.

If you don't see the swarm, you may discover termites only after they've done extensive damage to the structure of your house. You usually can't see termites eating because the part of the wood they like best is moist wood, and that's underneath. The outside may look just fine, but peel it away and there's a feast going on inside. During eating season, the termites look like this:

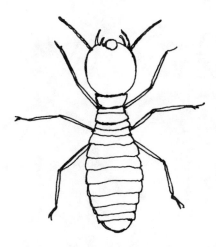

Don't panic when you see them. Termites are not necessarily hard to get rid of. The exterminator simply drills holes around the bottom of your house and fills them with a chemical that kills the termites by cutting them off from the ground. In effect, the chemicals form a moat of protection around the house. One application should be enough to cure the problem. The chemicals themselves, however, are a little scary. Some are suspected of causing cancer.

Exterminators are a little scary too. Local Better Business Bureaus report frequent complaints about crooked ones. In one scam, they call up and say: "Hello, I'm Harry Conman from the Sleazo Exterminator Company, and your neighborhood has been classified a termite red-alert area! You probably have termites, and unless you have us do some exterminating work here pretty soon, your house might fall down." This is bunk, because even if there really are termites around, it takes years of munching to do structural damage. I suggest that if someone tries to sell you a termite extermination, you should call two other exterminators (in the Yellow Pages) for opinions. Exterminators generally will inspect your house and give you an estimate for free. So there's no reason to take one company's word you need work done. Also, check on the company with your local Better Business Bureau.

Once you own a house, there are things you will need to do to protect it, and to keep it warm. Let's talk about protection first.

INSURANCE

The insurance companies don't make it simple. Maybe they figure if the policies were clearly written, we'd spend less, and they'd make less money.

The chart on page 54 shows the homeowner's policies four different insurance companies offer on a $75,000 house.

Price differences are often much greater than in this example, so it usually pays to call several companies before you buy. Note how much you save getting the $250 deductible. I think it's a better buy.

HO 1, HO 2, HO 3, etc., are the standard policies in the industry. There are not a lot of differences between them.

HO 1 is the basic minimum policy. You're covered in case of fire, windstorm, burglary, and vandalism. HO 2 also includes coverage for a collapsing roof, frozen or leaking pipes, falling objects, and a few other odds and ends. I'd buy HO 2; it only

POLICY
$75,000 Policy, Wood Frame House Long Island, N.Y.

	Travelers Insurance	Prudential Insurance	State Farm Insurance	Geico Insurance
Coverage on contents of the house	½ value of house	½ value of house	½ value of house	½ value of house
Personal liability	$25,000	$25,000	$100,000	$25,000
Guest medical payments (if a guest is injured)	$ 500	$ 500	$ 1,000	$ 500
Living expenses (for you, if your house is destroyed)	20% of policy ($15,000)	20% of policy ($15,000)	On HO1 + HO2 $15,000 On HO3-$22,500	HO1-10% of policy ($7,500) HO2 & 3—20% of policy ($15,000)
Detached structures (garages, sheds, etc.)	10% of policy ($7,500)	10% of policy ($7,500)	10% of policy ($7,500)	10% of policy ($7,500)
New-House discounts	Deduct 14% of base premium on new houses, 12% 1 yr., 10% 2 yr., 8% 3 yr., 6% 4 yr., 4% 5 yr., 2% 6 yr.	10% if house is 2 yrs. old or newer—varying discounts on houses up to 10 years	14% on new, down to 2% on 6 yrs.	10% if house is 5 yrs. old or newer
Discounts for safety features— smoke alarms, burglar alarms, dead-bolt locks, fire extinguishers	From 2% to 10%	None	From 2% to 15%	From 2% to 5%
COST: HO1—$100 deductible $250 deductible	$255 $212	$279 $223	$264 $237	$224 $202
HO2—$100 deductible $250 deductible	$324 $269	$339 $271	$331 $297	$310 $279
HO3—$100 deductible $250 deductible	$384 $310	$358 $286	$350 $315	$344 $310

costs a little more. HO 3 covers everything that's not specifically excluded in the fine print. They can put most anything in the fine print, so I'd stick with HO 2. HO 3 does, however, usually cover more. For example, if you spill paint on the carpet, HO 3 would cover it, since I doubt they'd have a clause excluding paint spills.

One warning: Insurance companies managed to slip a clever gimmick into homeowner's policies. Suppose you have $50,000 in insurance on your $100,000 house. If a fire did $20,000 damage to the house, you'd assume the insurance company owes you $20,000. Logical but, unfortunately, not true. Through a bizarre formula, the insurance company need pay you only $5/8$ of $20,000, or $12,500. You are entitled to the full $20,000 only if you had $80,000 coverage on your $100,000 house (80% coverage). I won't try to explain the logic behind this, but the moral is: Buy insurance for 80% of the value of your house.

SAVING ENERGY IN THE HOME

The obvious stuff (installing storm windows, turning down thermostats) you've heard about, and probably done by now. That leaves the more complicated decisions: do I have enough insulation? Is it worth the cost of ripping up the walls to put more insulation in? Do I need a new furnace, or some damper gadget on it? These are big money decisions, and most of us are way over our heads when we try to make them.

I could quote the experts and give you a long course in the physics of buildings and temperature. But this would bore you (and me) to death, and fortunately, there is no need. Thanks to a Department of Energy ruling, all utilities (gas and electric companies) must, as of January 1, 1981, give their customers "energy audits." Some have already started.

Energy audits are energy surveys of your home. The utility sends over one of its experts who pokes around your house— opening electric sockets to see into the walls (looking for insulation), checking attic and window heat loss, etc. Then they'll sit down and tell you what you need, what it might cost, and how much money you'll save if you follow their recommendation (see following example). Some improvements pay for themselves in just a few years. As a bonus, you get to deduct 15% of the cost from your taxes (up to $300). So save receipts.

The energy audit is one of the all-time great deals for the homeowner. It costs the utility at least $100 in labor and paperwork (Con Edison says its inspections cost $140 per home), yet most utilities will give you the inspection for no more than $10! $10 for $140 worth of work, lots of energy-saving advice, which you have no obligation to follow.

If you decide to follow the gas or electric company's suggestions, you'll have to pick the contractor. The utility will not arrange this for you, but the inspector will give you a list of "approved" contractors from which to choose. These contractors have no financial ties to the utility (the Energy Department didn't want any collusion: utilities recommending unnecessary work just to make money). The utility also does not guarantee the contractor's work, but the contractors know if the utility gets a lot of complaints about them, they'll be taken off the recom-

TYPICAL ENERGY AUDIT REPORT (Con Edison)

INSULATION COST AND SAVINGS SUMMARY

Item	Estimated Cost for Item (Dollars)	Estimated Annual Savings (Dollars)	Payback Period (Years)
Water-heater insulation blanket	$ 28	$ 15	1.86
Door-weatherstripping	44	17	2.58
Clock-thermostat installation	120	28	4.29
Floor insulation, including access holes	552	105	5.25
Ceiling insulation, including vents	410	47	8.72
Wall insulation	1,585	135	11.74

mended list, and they'll lose all that good business. So they have an incentive to do good work.

Even if you don't plan to make energy improvements immediately, call your utility soon to request the audit. Most utilities don't have many inspectors, so it takes them months to get to your house.

Some private companies offer to take infrared pictures of your house to tell you if you have enough insulation. These pictures reveal how much heat is leaking from your house, and where the leaks are. The pictures cost about $125 and are worth it.

One test mentioned earlier that you can do yourself: On a cold day, stand in the corners of several rooms, putting one hand on a wall that faces outdoors, the other hand on an interior wall. If the interior wall is noticeably warmer, there's not enough insulation.

INSULATION

If you do add insulation, your choices are Fiberglas batts, cellulose fill or urea-formaldehyde foam. All have advantages and disadvantages.

Fiberglas batts: This is the cheapest insulation, and what you'd use if you put insulation in yourself. The batts are soft Fiberglas (see Illustration) made of glass that's melted, then spun into yarn, and woven into layers about 6 inches thick. You buy the Fiberglas in rolls, cut it to size, and just tack it to your attic floor or wherever you need it. It's easy. Anyone can do it. The problem with Fiberglas is that if your house is already built, you can only put the batts into exposed areas (attic, basement ceilings, etc.). You can't get them into walls without ripping the walls apart.

Try not to inhale Fiberglas particles. There's a question as to what they may do to your health.

Both cellulose fill and urea-formaldehyde foam can be put into existing walls. This is no do-it-yourself job. Professional insulating contractors (under "Insulation" in the Yellow Pages) drill holes from the outside and pump the insulation in.

Cellulose fill: This is the cheaper of the two. It's nothing but shredded paper treated with boric acid (to make it fire resistant).

Urea-Formaldehyde Foam: Formaldehyde foam looks and feels much like shaving cream. After it's pumped into the walls, it hardens into something akin to Styrofoam plastic. Foam costs more but you make it up in heating bills. The actual installation price depends on the size of your house, and how much insulation it has already. Brick and stucco houses cost more because they're harder to drill into than wood houses. Aluminum siding is rough too, because the insulator must remove all the siding before he can drill into the house.

There's one scary problem with foam insulation. Some people claim it is poisonous.

In Bayville, New Jersey, Mike and Josephine Wagner had their house insulated with urea-formaldehyde foam. They noticed no unusual smells, but several days later, their son's piano teacher suddenly complained, "I can't stay here." "What's the matter?" asked Josephine Wagner.

"Can't you smell it?" exclaimed the teacher, her eyes tearing. "I can't breathe!"

A neighbor who came to visit said, "I don't know how you can stand it here; it's horrible."

Apparently, the foam had not hardened properly. Some of the formaldehyde was evaporating, and the gas flowed into the house. The Wagners, exposed gradually, had failed to notice the smell, but they soon started developing health problems. First their son complained of headaches and watery eyes. Then his sister developed the same symptoms, and even the dog got sick. Mike Wagner said when he called the contractor he was told, "Open your windows, and the odor will gradually disappear."

It didn't. The effects became worse. Mike Wagner, a schoolteacher, fainted while in class, and he was unable to continue teaching. Today he gets dizzy when he comes into contact with various chemicals. The last time he went to a fast-food restaurant, he passed out and had to be hospitalized. His doctor believes he is reacting to the smell of the plastic carton in which the hamburger is served.

Today, two years after it was insulated, the Wagners' house stands empty. Whenever the family tries to return, they become sick. They live in a rented home.

The Wagners are suing the insulation contractor. The lawsuit probably will drag on for years. The contractor says he did nothing wrong; he maintains that he did not put in too much formaldehyde, and he mixed it properly. His lawyer accuses the Wagners of lying.

Plenty of other people have had the same problem. At this writing, one state has banned foam insulation. If you already have had your house insulated with the U-F foam, be alert for the symptoms of formaldehyde poisoning: difficult breathing, watery eyes, dizziness, headache. These symptoms are most likely to occur during hot, humid weather, or when your home's central heating or air-conditioning goes on. The symptoms may come and go, and you may think you just have the flu. If you have questions about it, the U.S. Consumer Product Safety Commission has a toll-free hotline for U-F foam-insulating problems: 800-638-8326. (In Maryland, 800-492-8363; in Alaska, Hawaii, Puerto Rico and the Virgin Islands, 800-638-8333.)

The U-F foam industry says the formaldehyde problem is exaggerated. When there is odor, says the National Association of Urea-Formaldehyde Foam Insulation Manufacturers, it's because a fly-by-night contractor has mixed the stuff badly, and that happens fewer than ½0th of 1% of the time. "It's a fine product," says an industry spokesman. "It's a shame we've had all these bad raps because we could save a lot of energy with our product."

That is also true. It's something you must decide for yourself. Millions of homes have been insulated with U-F foam without any problems.

Sometimes health problems arise simply because people have sealed leaks in their homes. It's another "bad news from good" story. You weatherstrip the last leaky door, and proudly count up the money you're going to save. Then everyone in the family gets sick. The cause: indoor pollution. Gases from cigarettes, stoves, cleaning products, etc., no longer escape from the house, because the measures you've taken to keep the cold air out also trapped the bad air in. There's no real solution to this, but for your safety, you should be aware of the warning symptoms: burning eyes, headache and exhaustion. You may have to undo some of your weatherproofing.

OTHER ENERGY-SAVING TIPS

Most fireplaces waste more heat than they create. Fire needs air, so it sucks cold in from the outside, and then sends most of the hot air up the chimney. New heat-efficient fireplaces radiate more heat in the room, but they have glass doors that make the fire a little less romantic. If you already have a fireplace, there are grates you can install to make it more heat efficient. The grates are steel tubes that take cold air from the room, circulate it through the fire, and then blow the now-hot air back into the room. Fireplace stores sell the blower grates for about $100.

Most fireplace flue dampers don't seal the chimney completely, so you waste some room heat when the fireplace is not in use. You can reduce this heat loss by putting a solid screen or curtain in front of the fireplace. Fireplace stores sell glass screens for $30 to $300; $300 is for fancy looks, the $30 type works just as well. Cheaper yet is a fireplace curtain for $9. The curtain is a piece of canvas that hooks on to the front of the fireplace to seal off the air flow. One disadvantage: Since the curtain is flammable canvas, you have to wait until the fire is completely out before attaching the curtain.

Princeton University researchers have found that people often insulate the whole house and then lose some of the heat savings to the attic. There are rarely gaping holes in the ceiling, but if you crawl around the attic (it may help to turn off the lights and look for light from below), you may find holes made during installation of wiring or plumbing. By stuffing in some Fiberglas from a Fiberglas batt, you'll stop the leak.

OTHER INSULATION TIPS

Don't press down on Fiberglas insulation. Squeezing it makes it insulate less.

Don't put insulation on the ceiling of an unheated attic. This may trap moisture and cause the wood to rot. If you have an unheated attic, insulate the floor of the attic, not the walls or the roof.

To see if windows or doorways are leaking cold air, hold a candle near them. If the flame flickers, do some caulking. Caulking guns, available in hardware stores, are easy to use and much cheaper than heating oil.

If you're buying cellulose or foam insulation, check around your home while it is being installed. At one house, installers kept pouring foam in. "I can't believe the walls aren't full yet," said the contractor. Finally he looked downstairs. The entire basement was filled with foam (there was a hole in the basement wall).

Save receipts; in some cases, insulation entitles you to a tax credit.

In the House

MAJOR APPLIANCES AND FURNISHINGS

So you're in the market for a refrigerator, washer–dryer, etc.? Which do you choose? How can you cut the cost of running them? Since models are always changing, the best guide is *Consumer Reports* because it keeps updating its tests. Any library has the back issues, or simpler: the annual *Buying Guide* that summarizes the *Consumer Reports* monthly findings.

Now consider energy use. When trying to save electricity, it makes sense to cut back more on some applicances than others. You can run one hundred electric shavers or sixty electric can openers for less money than it costs to run a clothes dryer on hot. Appliances that generate heat or cold use far more energy than those that use the electricity just to run a motor. That's why a dripping hot-water faucet is so expensive; over a year, the electricity to heat that water might cost you $100.

When buying a big appliance that generates heat or cold, a mistake can cost you, unbelievably, *thousands* of dollars.

REFRIGERATORS

The manufacturer doesn't care how much energy the refrigerator uses because he's not paying for it; we are. He only wants to make the machine as cheaply as possible so he can sell more of them. He knows that most of us are uninformed about energy costs; we'll run into the store and buy the cheapest model that meets our size requirements. If he can make his refrigerator $20 cheaper by taking out some insulation and using a cheap compressor, why not? The consumer can't see how much insulation is in the walls.

WHAT IT COSTS TO RUN ELECTRICAL APPLIANCES

Appliance	Costs per hour: 10¢ per kilowatt-hour rate
Refrigerators:	
12 cu ft manual defrost	.91¢
14 cu ft cycle manual defrost	1.57¢
14 cu ft frost free	1.83¢
18 cu ft frost free	2.28¢
Freezers:	
15 cu ft chest manual defrost	1.58¢
16 cu ft upright manual defrost	2.1¢
16 cu ft upright frost free	3.0¢
Toaster (GE 900 Watt)	9.0¢
Blender (Waring household)	.36¢
Radio (GE clock radio)	.08¢
Toaster Oven (GE 1350 Watt)	13.5¢
(GE 1500 Watt)	15.0¢
Conair Home Hair Dryer	15.0¢
Space Heater for 12 x 12 room	15.0¢
Clothes Dryer (Maytag home) (4500 watt)	45.0¢
Electric Shaver (Schick)	.47¢
Powerful Stereo (Yamaha M-4)	4.7¢
Ordinary Stereo	3.8¢
Can Opener (Farberware 248B)	.85¢
Television (B&W)	2.5¢
(Color)	3.33¢
Light Bulb (100 Watt)	1.0¢
(60 Watt)	.6¢
(25 Watt)	.25¢
Air Conditioner	15.1¢
Electric Blanket	1.2¢
Vacuum Cleaner	6.3¢
Iron	5.6¢
Fan	2.0¢
Washing Machine	4.0¢
Food Processor	3.6¢

Source: Con Edison

Don't fall for the "cheap" sell. Figure the cost of *running* the machine in with the list price. A refrigerator costs, over its ten- to twenty-year lifetime, more to run than to buy. Some models currently on sale (especially the cheaper ones) will use $2,000 more in electricity than others. Refrigerators today use a lot of power because they not only have to cool the food, they also have to cool the heaters in the freezer walls (that's right, there are heaters in the walls; that's what keeps the frost from gathering in frost-free refrigerators). Some companies now make energy-saving models that will save you hundreds of dollars a year in electricity costs. They cost a little more to buy (maybe $600 vs. $535), but it's well worth it. Be careful, however: not all that say "energy saving" are really energy savers, and having an "energy saver" switch doesn't mean much—the switch just saves you a few bucks by occasionally turning off the de-froster.

What you should look for is the "energy label." All big appliances made after June 1980 carry labels that tell you how much electricity they use. The labels are not complicated (this is amazing, considering that they were designed by a U.S. government agency); each states clearly how much electricity (in dollars) that appliance is likely to use in one year. The dollar calculation is based on electricity costing 5¢ per kilowatt hour. If you live where electricity costs more (we Con Ed customers pay 11¢), you must multiply the dollar amount accordingly.

A few more energy tips:

1. A full refrigerator uses less electricity than an empty one. The food helps store the cold.

2. Top-freezer models use less electricity than side-by-side types because they leak less cold when you open the door.

3. In the back, or at the bottom, of your refrigerator is a bunch of coils. Clean them three times a year (*unplug* the refrigerator first; then use a vacuum) and you'll save about $15 a year.

When deciding what size refrigerator to buy, I think 16 cubic feet is plenty for a family of two, 19 cubic feet for a family of four. Add 2 feet if you do a lot of entertaining.

Many people find side-by-side refrigerators convenient. They are more expensive to buy, however, and as I said before, more expensive to run. Before you buy one, make sure you have enough room in your kitchen for the two doors to swing open freely.

On to other appliances:

FREEZERS

They're not the money-savers they're touted to be. Okay, maybe if you bought meat in bulk at great bargains and froze it, you *might* save more than the freezer and its electricity cost you. But most of us save much less than we think buying meat in bulk (see page 90), and most of us tend to forget what we've stored and so some of what we put in the freezer ends up going to waste.

If you do buy a freezer, you have a choice of two types: upright and chest (opens from the top). The upright is most convenient—the shelves are easy to see. However, uprights also cost more and use more electricity. Chest freezers burn less electricity because cold sinks; less escapes when you open the door. Chest freezers also need defrosting less often.

Before you put food in your freezer, I suggest you read "Storing Food," page 93.

MICROWAVE OVENS

Why not? I think the safety problem is overblown. The worry is that the ovens leak radiation. True, no one knows if long-term exposure to microwaves is harmful, and maybe we'll soon learn horrible things about such exposure. But the government's rules on how much radiation the ovens may leak are pretty tough. In fact they're so tough, you're exposed to far more microwaves using your CB radio.

If you're worried about your microwave oven leaking too much, buy a leakage tester. Appliance stores sell them for about $30.

Cooking by microwave is an entirely different style of cooking. *Advantages:*

Speed. Food cooks faster by microwave. You can defrost in a fraction of the time.

Taste. Some foods dry out less in microwave.

Energy Saving. About $15 per year.

Convenience. Microwaves pass through paper, plastic, and glass without heating them, so you can cook in most anything, and then serve on that same dish. That's great for leftovers, which can be refrigerated, quickly reheated, and served on the same plate. And microwave reheating doesn't dry foods like a conventional oven does.

Disadvantages:

No Browning. The microwave advantage, cooking food evenly, is a disadvantage when it comes to browning a roast, or putting a dark crust on baked goods. Newer microwave ovens have added electric heaters so you can give the roast a blast of electricity at the end and brown it that way. But some people say it just doesn't taste the same.

Change of Habit. You will have to re-learn your cooking techniques; old recipes may not work in a microwave oven. Microwave ovens tend to steam food, rather than make them crisp. Pizza and french fries come out soggy. Vegetables tend to be crisper.

AIR-CONDITIONERS

The important thing in buying an air-conditioner is to get the right size. Not just for energy saving, but because if you get one that's too big for a room, it cools the room long before it sucks the humidity out. Then you're stuck with a cold but clammy room. If the machine is too small for the room, it wastes energy working too hard and may never get the room comfortably cool.

The formula for determining the proper size machine is unpleasantly complicated. But the alternative is to guess. or to ask a salesperson to guess for you. That can result in wasted money and an uncomfortable room. So it pays to be precise. Here are the calculations you should make:

1. Multiply the room's width (in feet) by length and then by 8 (W × L × 8).

2. If the room has another room above it or if it's well insulated, multiply that by 10 (W × L × 8 × 10).

If there's only a roof or an unheated attic above it, multiply it by 18 (W × L × 8 × 18).

3. If the longest outside wall faces north, multiply the whole mess by 16 (W × L × 8 × 10 × 16).

If the longest outside wall faces east, multiply by 17 (W × L × 8 × 10 × 17.).

If the longest outside wall faces south, multiply by 18 (W × L × 8 × 10 × 18).

If the longest outside wall faces west, multiply by 20 (W × L × 8 × 10 × 20).

If the longest outside wall is shaded by trees or another building, multiply by 16 (W × L × 8 × 10 × 16).

4. Divide the total by 60 ($\frac{W \times L \times 8 \times 10 \times 17}{60}$) and that's the number of BTUs you need.

There's a more complicated formula. It takes more time, but the answer will be more precise. Write to the Association of Home Appliance Manufacturers, 20 N. Wacker Dr., Chicago, Illinois 60606. They'll mail you a free "cooling load estimate form."

LIGHTING

Some changes could save you $30 a year. You probably know fluorescent lights use less electricity; the problem is that their harsh light isn't great for romance. Now they sell tinted fluorescents, which solve much of the problem, but even without the tint, the fluorescent glare doesn't bother most people in their kitchens and bathrooms. The savings are considerable: fluorescents give as much light for one-third the cost.

Some companies now sell "extended life" or "long-life" bulbs. Don't be fooled. These are not energy bargains; they use more electricity than ordinary bulbs; so, even though you replace them less often, they will cost you more in the long run. On the other hand, they do save *human* energy. If you have a bulb that's out of the way and a real pain to change, the long-life bulb is a great convenience.

You've probably heard that flicking lights on and off burns extra electricity, so it's better to just keep them on if you leave for an hour. That's a myth. There is no surge of electricity when you flick on an ordinary light, and only a mild surge when you turn on a fluorescent light. So, it's *always* better to turn out an ordinary light, and with fluorescents, it pays to leave them on only if you plan to return to the room within three minutes.

One 60-watt bulb costs you about $50 in electricity if it's left on for a full year. With the price of electricity going bananas, can you save money lighting candles instead? Sorry, no. To produce the same amount of light, candles will cost you four times as much as electric light. But for those of you who like using candles, here's a tip: to make candles last a little longer, store them in the refrigerator. Then they'll burn more slowly because the cold wax evaporates more slowly. Don't overdo a good idea and put them in the freezer; they'll dry out and crack.

GUARANTEES. OR IS IT WARRANTIES?

There's no difference between guarantee and warranty. "Warranty" was probably invented by a pompous manufacturer who decided "guarantee" didn't sound impressive enough. Why not? If doctors can call bleeding "hemorrhaging," why shouldn't manufacturers call a guarantee a warranty?

Today the law requires warranties be either "full" or "limited." This hampers the con game advertising of "3-YEAR WARRANTY" and then saying in the fine print that repairs are free only if the product is damaged by an aardvark or if it falls into a volcano. Forcing manufacturers to say "limited warranty" tips you off that there are limits to the coverage, so you can take the trouble to read the fine print. A "full warranty" means the manufacturer promises to fix any defect free and fix it without putting you to a *lot* of trouble. In other words, you may have to bring an iron to the store to have it fixed, but you don't have to cart in your dishwasher—the repair-person comes to you. Under a full warranty, if they can't fix the appliance, they must replace it, or return your money. (This is why the automakers now offer limited warranties; they don't want to have to replace a car when they can't fix it.)

A manufacturer is not required to offer any warranty, but all products carry an "implied warranty." That means a product must do what it's supposed to do: a reclining chair must recline, a toaster must toast. If they don't, you have a legal right to a refund. *Getting* the refund is another matter; a lawyer will cost you more than the product. Fortunately, you don't need a lawyer to take the manufacturer to small claims court (see page 201).

Appliance dealers now sell "service contracts." You pay maybe $200, and they promise free repairs. Don't take it. Odds are that you won't have $200 worth of repairs during the contract period. If it was likely that you would, why would they sell you the service contract?

One last tip: you know the little warranty card you're supposed to send in? It's bunk. You can throw it away and the warranty is still good; all you need is a sales receipt. Often the card is used as a way for the manufacturer to get more information about you, sometimes so he can send you junk mail. The card has nothing to do with the legality of the warranty.

SEALS OF APPROVAL

Anybody can come up with a "Seal of Approval" and some-times most anybody does. "Approved by the Consumer Experiment Institute" was put on one product; the Institute turned out to be the manufacturer itself.

We've all seen the UL seal. It's one seal that actually means something. It means the product has passed tests given by Underwriters Laboratories, a nonprofit organization. Manufac-turers know the UL stamp of approval helps their products to sell, so they pay to submit their products to UL's tests. If they pass, they get the seal; if they flunk, they probably still sell the product, but without the seal.

The tests are pretty good. UL does things like check hinges on refrigerator doors by having machines open and close the doors 300,000 times. Coffeepots must pass tilt tests so they don't spill too easily. The seal, however, is only a piece of advice; it is not a guarantee. Nor are the tests foolproof. The U.S. Consumer Products Safety Commission found thousands of fire-prone TV sets carrying the UL seal. Some companies get the seal for their product and then take shortcuts in manufacturing, making an inferior product. UL makes surprise factory inspections to catch offenders, but it can't police every single product.

BEDS

Regular Beds. Just try them out. Don't hesitate to flop around on several in the store. After all, you're going to spend a lot of time on the one you buy, so it better be the firmness you like. A hard bed is better for back problems.

Waterbeds. If you're buying a new bed, consider a waterbed. They're actually cheaper than regular beds. I used to have one and would still have one, if my landlord hadn't found out. Everyone I've interviewed about the waterbeds likes them. I think most people who joke about seasickness and sloshing sounds haven't tried sleeping in them. Waterbeds are comfortable, fun, and cool in the summer (warm in the winter, too; you adjust the heater). You can sleep with your arm around someone and your hand doesn't go to sleep. Some hospitals use them for immobile patients so they don't get bedsores.

Waterbeds are not so dangerous as they may seem. Leaks are rare, and when there is a leak, the protective liner holds the water in until you patch the hole. There are no geysers (as in situation comedies); one store let me stab a few beds with a screwdriver to show how small the leaks would be. Indeed, the leak was mild, and they fixed it in five minutes with a repair kit.

My landlord told me either the waterbed or I would have to go because he was worried about the weight. So you'd better check your lease if you live in an apartment building. In truth, the weight problem isn't that serious because waterbeds weigh no more per square foot than a refrigerator. On the other hand, they are heavier than regular beds, so I'd think twice before buying one for a very old house. One guy put one in his houseboat and the houseboat sank.

Simple waterbeds cost about $200. That includes frame, water bag and heater. You need a heater, because without it the water will be room temperature (say 70°), which feels freezing cold because your skin temperature is 90°. If you're reluctant to buy without trying one first, many hotels have them; check in and have a test sleep. As I said, everyone I know who has tried them, likes them. Even my cats.

SMALL APPLIANCES—TELEPHONES, SMOKE DETECTORS

Hooray for technology. Toasters, blenders, hair dryers, electric coffeepots, irons, etc., today work better and cost less in real (adjusted for inflation) dollars than in past years. I suggest reading *Consumer Reports* for brand advice, but there aren't many differences between brands. In fact, different brands are sometimes manufactured by the same company. The company just wants to *seem* to be giving the consumer more choices.

Be wary of the "miracle" small appliances advertised during late-night TV shows ("Send away for the automatic salad tosser!"). The New York State Consumer Protection Board sent away for dozens of such products. Almost none really did what it was advertised to do.

TELEPHONES

Most of us rent our phones from Ma Bell (or whatever local phone company services your area), although renting is a stupid waste of money. A few years ago it became legal to buy your own phone, and if you analyze the costs, buying your own is by far the better deal. Example: Renting a Trimline ® phone from New York Telephone costs about $69 a year, yet you can buy your own just like it for as little as $69 at some discount stores. So the first year you break even, then you start saving $69 a year.

Most homes today have jacks. You don't have to know how to

wire anything, you just take the phone home and plug it in. If you have the old jacks at home, which look like this,

you'll need to buy a converter. The store that sold you the phone will sell you one for about $5. If you don't have a jack, you'll have to have a Bell technician install one; that costs about $40, extra jacks about $15.*

When owning your own phone became legal, Ma Bell quickly opened up its own PhoneCenter Stores, advertising them as a bargain. This is ridiculous. These stores are a bargain only when compared to Ma Bell's other expensive services. For example, they sell you a Mickey Mouse phone for about $100, but you don't really own it. You only own the plastic casing. The inside mechanism still belongs to Ma Bell, which means they still stick you with the monthly rent. The only way you save buying at the phone company's PhoneCenter Store is if you were going to rent from Ma Bell anyway; picking up your own phone at the store saves you a $13.25 installation charge.

Opening its own stores was a brilliant bit of marketing on Ma Bell's part. The stores fool people into thinking they are getting the same bargain available at private stores. The only benefit of renting or buying from Ma Bell is that Ma Bell pays for repairs. But phones don't need repairing very often.

Assuming you now rent your own phones, and I have just convinced you you'll be better off buying your own, here's what you need to do:

1. Note the type of jacks you have (if any).
2. Go to any private phone-selling store, pick out the phones you want, and tell them what kind of jack you have. The store

---

* These prices refer to New York Telephone rates and vary from state to state.

will then sell you the proper connection, or tell you what to do if you don't have jacks.

3. Call the phone company and tell them you've bought your own phones, so they should come and pick up their rental phones. (You save some money if you bring the rental phones in yourself.) The phone company will ask you what type of phones you bought; the law says you must tell them, so the bureaucrats can register everything properly. You will still have to pay the phone company a monthly fee for using their lines, but your overall bill will be much lower.

4. Plug in your phones. Call your friends long distance; you can afford it because of all the money you just saved.

Another Money-Saving Idea: If you have a push-button phone, and make a lot of long-distance calls, you can lower your phone bill by subscribing to "Sprint." For $10 a month, Sprint subscribers can call long distance for about half what Ma Bell charges. You punch in a special code (that's why you need a push-button phone), then direct dial whomever you want to call. Savings range from 25% to 50% (depending on what time you make the call).

Restrictions:

1. Sprint operates only during nonbusiness hours. That means all day Saturday, Sunday, and holidays, but only at night during the week.

2. Sprint operates only in the biggest 80 metropolitan areas. That includes most of us, but not all of us.

For Sprint to save you money, you have to make at least $25 worth of nonbusiness-hour long-distance calls during the month. Sprint, Box 974, Burlingame, California 94010; 415-692-5600.

SMOKE DETECTORS

Every home should have one. They're cheap: $40 is the average price. Hardware stores sell them.

Thirty-three Americans die in fires every day. Do you think you'll wake up if there's a fire in your house? The smoke, maybe the noise will startle you awake? No way. In fact, smoke acts as a drug that puts you into a deeper sleep. Smoke usually kills you before the fire even gets close. And most bad fires occur at night, when a heater, cigarette or Christmas tree starts the blaze unnoticed.

The alarms are very simple. You don't have to wire them up or anything. Just plug in the electric ones; stick a battery in the battery-powered ones. To install them, screw them to the wall or ceiling. You don't even have to do that much; I'm so lazy I have mine balanced on top of a bookcase. Don't put one too near the kitchen or it will go off every time you cook.

There's not much difference between the battery-powered and plug-in models. Battery-powered ones usually have an alarm that warns you when the batteries are dying. In any case, you can check them periodically with the smoke from a cigarette. They all work. Buy one.

If you have a big apartment or a house, buy two. Or three. A good place to put one is the top of the stairway.

ESCAPE LADDERS

Alright, the smoke alarm goes off, you spring awake, only to find the fire has blocked the stairs, and you can't go down. The only escape: the second-floor bedroom window. Fortunately, you've just bought an escape ladder. "Easy exit! Protect your family," says the ad. It's a little like a rope ladder, but the rungs are metal. You pull it out from under the bed, anchor one end to the windowsill, throw the rest out, and start to climb down.

But now you're in trouble. Rope ladders are great for climbing into tree houses or helicopters, but they're bad news when you're climbing out of houses. The problem: A rope ladder lies flat against the wall—there's no room for your toes—when you try to climb down, your feet slip off the rungs, and you end up hanging by your hands. I tried it with several brands of escape ladders. The first scary part is climbing out the window and trying to find the rungs with your feet. The next scary part is realizing there's not enough room for your feet, and you're going to have to climb using your hands alone. I was able to do that because I'm relatively strong, and was anticipating the problem, but *Consumer Reports* found most people couldn't climb down that way, and so for them, escape probably would have meant falling. *Consumer Reports,* therefore, rated 7 escape ladders "not acceptable."

The solution: buy an escape ladder that has little braces that push the ladder away from the wall (see pictures).

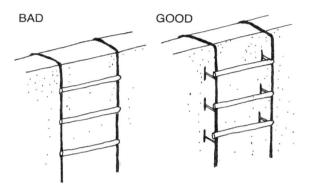

BAD   GOOD

If your hardware store doesn't carry them, you can order one from G.A.M.A. Inc., Framingham, Massachusetts 01701. They call it the "Exitable." Rival Mfg., 36th and Bennington, Kansas City, Missouri 64129, sells one called the "Rival Firescape."

Escape ladders cost $30 to $80. When you order, tell them whether you need a second- or third-floor model.

CHRISTMAS TREES

If you are buying a real tree, look for that deep-green color, because that means it's fresh. But be careful: some dealers spray trees with green dye! So, the best freshness test is to tap the butt of the tree on the ground. Only a few needles should fall off. Also, bend a needle; fresh needles bend, old ones break.

Leave the tree outdoors until right before decorating. Every second indoors shortens the tree's green period. Before you put the tree in the stand, saw an inch or two off the stem at a slight angle. This opens the pores so the tree can drink better. If you keep the tree in water, it should last two weeks. There are products you can buy to keep the tree fresh longer; however the U.S. Consumer Product Safety Commission says they don't work.

Christmas tree fires kill dozens of people every winter. If you keep the tree watered, however, it is remarkably fire resistant. Nearly all plastic trees are fire resistant today. Notice I say fire resistant, not fireproof. All trees will burn if the fire is hot enough. That's a good reason to get rid of opened Christmas wrappings as soon as possible. Turn off the tree lights when you either leave the house or go to sleep. A hot light sitting on a dry branch starts many of the fires.

CARPETS

It's tough to give advice about carpets because the quality differences are so subtle you have to be an expert to tell good from not so good. The only simple guide: better carpets have more fibers per inch.

TYPES:

Nylon: Most carpets sold today are made of nylon. It's sturdy stuff, has good soil resistance, and bears up well in heavy traffic areas like stairways and hallways. It tends to look a little shiny. Cost: $8 to $25* per square yard.

Polyester: It's usually softer and fluffier than nylon, but it mats down faster after being walked on. It's not so strong as nylon. Cost: $8 to $20.*

Wool: The best. Wears the longest. Of course, costs the most: typically $22 to $35,* up to $80* for some patterns.

Olefin: Thin, but the most stain-resistant carpet. Great if you have kids or pets. Cost: from $5 to $15.*

Acrylic: Looks and feels much like wool, but costs less. Tends to "pill" and form fuzzy balls of fiber after hard wear, however. Cost: from $5 to $20.*

* Installation not included—installation usually costs from $3.50 to $4.50 per square yard.

Always get a carpet pad. It goes under the carpet, and makes the carpet feel softer and last longer. Carpet pads come in foam rubber or natural fiber; rubber is better in most areas because it won't mildew.

You save about $4 a yard if you install carpet yourself. Other advantages:

1. You lay the carpet whenever you want, instead of waiting around for the installers.

2. You will take extra precautions around furniture and walls that the installers won't. After all, you live there; they don't.

Disadvantages:

1. If you have any strange-shaped rooms or stairways to carpet, it will be hard for you to cut and fit the carpet correctly. You need tools: a sharp-edged knife to cut the carpet, and two-sided tape or tackless strips. A tackless strip is a piece of tape with tacks sticking out of it (it's easier than using individual tacks). The tape holds the tacks in position. You don't need the strip once the tacks are in because it's buried in the carpet.

MOVING AND STORAGE

Moving is miserable. I don't know anyone who's had what they would call a "good experience" moving. Something almost always goes wrong.

The following is a typical moving adventure. The problems are numbered so we can discuss them individually afterward:

It starts nicely. You call three movers for estimates. The movers are pleasant, provide estimates, and give you useful advice. You pick the one with the lowest estimate. They say they'll be there Monday morning to pack your stuff, and they'll have it in Dallas by Wednesday.

You get up at dawn Monday, so you'll be ready when the movers arrive, but they don't arrive until afternoon. At five they say, "Sorry, that's the end of the workday, we'll finish packing tomorrow." You stay at Aunt Edna's because all your night stuff is packed. Tuesday they finish the job, weigh the truck and say,

"Looks like you've added some furniture since the estimate, the bill's gonna be $600 more than we said."

"To hell with you," you say. "The estimate was only $1,200!"

"Tough luck, buddy, the estimate means doddlysquat. Anyway, we've got your furniture in the truck, so what're you gonna do about it now?" [1]

Nothing, you decide. You immediately start driving to Dallas, so that you'll be in your new house by Wednesday noon, the time the movers say they will arrive. When you are still waiting at 5 P.M. you call the moving company headquarters to ask why the movers haven't arrived [2].

"Oh, there was some kind of delay," says the dispatcher, "they will be there tomorrow morning." You pack up the kids, and go to a motel [3]. Jimmy spills catsup on his clothes, and all his others are in the moving van. The movers don't come Thursday, or Friday either. The company explains that because you're moving in July, there's a shortage of drivers, and the van won't get there until Saturday [4]. No luck Saturday, but they do arrive Monday.

They unpack. You notice big scratches on your brand-new dining-room table, and dents in your antique desk. You complain, and the mover shows you the inventory sheet. "Table, 4 sc, g, 2 bu, ch." it sez. "That means 4 scratches, 1 gouge, 2 burn marks, and 1 chipped place. See," sez the mover, "this stuff was already scratched before we picked it up." "It was not!" you scream, but you are out of luck because you already okayed the inventory sheet, because you didn't know what 4 sc, g, 2 bu, ch meant [5]. Later you learn 3 valuable pictures and some silverware are missing altogether. You complain, and the mover says there's no record of them on the inventory, and therefore they never existed [6]. You swear, sign the inventory sheet, and tell the movers to get lost. Later you notice other furniture has been damaged, but when you complain, the mover points out that you signed the inventory sheet, and therefore you have accepted the goods "as is" and have no right to complain.

To analyze by the numbers:

[1] There's nothing you can do about the rise in price once they've got your furniture. Moving companies sometimes give

super-low estimates just to get your business. Be wary of estimates that are *much* lower than those of other companies. Moving rates vary, but not by a lot; a super-low rate suggests a shady company. Estimates are free, so you might as well get several.

Sometimes people hide some of their furniture at estimate time thinking they can trick the mover. This is pointless. The estimate is just an estimate; it is not binding. You'll pay for whatever the stuff actually weighs. Hiding things just cheats you out of an accurate estimate.

Once your furniture is in the truck and weighed, you can check to see if they are cheating you on the weight. They weigh the truck full, and weigh it again after it's unloaded. If you're suspicious about the bill, simply notify the mover (call the company, not the driver; the driver will just get angry) that you want a re-weigh. The company will call you when the truck gets to your area, and you can arrange to meet the truck at a weigh station. It's a good precaution. Sometimes movers bribe the weighmaster to raise the weight. He won't if you're there. You have to pay about $20 for a re-weigh if the weight is within 120 pounds of the original weigh. It seldom is. Even without cheating, scales are variable enough that 120 pounds differences are common. When there's a re-weigh, the mover can charge you only for the lighter of the two, so requesting a re-weigh is almost always worth the $20. It could save you hundreds of dollars.

[2] Movers are sometimes late picking up; they are *often* late delivering. There's nothing you can do except to be aware it might happen. Then you'll at least be flexible about your plans. Jimmy will have spare clothes.

[3] The moving company must pay for reasonable living expenses if a delivery is late. Reasonable means motel and ½ your restaurant costs (they figure you would have paid to eat anyway). Save receipts.

[4] July is peak season and you are more likely to be hit by delays. In fact, peak season is mid-May through September, when kids are out of school. During those months, 60% of the moves are made. If you can arrange to make your move during

the winter, you're much better off. There will be more trucks, and more experienced people. Some companies (usually smaller ones) even give discounts during the off season. During the summer, moving companies hire lots of part-timers who know little about handling delicate furniture.

[5] The inventory sheet is very important. It lists everything that's in the truck, and its condition.

Here's what the symbols stand for:

BE	bent	G	gouged
BR	broken	MI	mildew
BU	burned	MO	motheaten
CH	chipped	SC	scratched
CU	contents and condition unknown	T	torn
D	dented	W	badly worn
		Z	cracked

You have to watch the movers, because they tend to throw in a few SC, BE, BUs, etc., after everything. It's a pain to check their notations, but unless you do, they will claim everything was already dented.

[6] If it's not on the inventory, you have no legal right to complain if it's missing later. It's a good idea to make your own inventory list before the movers arrive, so you can check your list against the movers'. This will catch items left off the list accidentally (or on purpose).

When you take delivery DON'T SIGN THE INVENTORY unless you're satisfied that everything is there, and undamaged. Once you sign, you're stuck. If something is damaged, mark "damaged" on the inventory. If you mark it on the inventory, the movers are pretty good about paying.

If you have problems, call 800-336-3094. That's the toll-free number of a moving company group. They represent the companies, but they nevertheless will give you useful advice. They will also arbitrate complaints.

You can also write the ICC, which regulates moving companies (12th and Constitution Avenue, N.W., Washington, D.C.

20423. 202-275-7252). The ICC does not regulate small companies that move only within states.

The ICC requires movers to report how often they make very inaccurate estimates, how often they are late in showing up, and how often they damage goods. The ICC also tallies the complaints that come directly to the ICC. However, the ICC, not known for its consumer helpfulness, has not made much of an effort to give this useful data to the public. I think it should, since complaints help predict which companies are most and least likely to cause problems. Since the ICC doesn't publicize the list, I will:

THE ICC'S COMPLAINT RATIOS FOR HOUSEHOLD MOVERS, 1978

		COMPLAINTS		
			Per 100	
	Ship-		Ship-	
Company	ments	To ICC	ments	Rank
Aero Mayflower Transit	128,543	3,687	2.9	13
Allied Van Lines	218,382	3,018	1.4	6-tie
American Red Ball	24,640	624	2.5	11
Andrews Van Lines	6,390	69	1.1	3
Atlas Van Lines	69,711	813	1.2	4-tie
Bekins Van Lines	101,504	2,313	2.3	10-tie
Burnham Van Service	17,414	125	.7	1-tie
Fernstrom Storage	2,094	28	1.3	5
Global Van Lines	39,738	804	2.0	8
King Van Lines	13,547	291	2.1	9
Lyon Moving and Storage	30,204	214	.7	1-tie
National Van Lines	10,699	291	2.7	12
Neptune World Wide Moving	5,496	45	.8	2
North American Van Lines	122,684	2,838	2.3	10-tie
Smyth Van Lines	18,522	267	1.4	6-tie
Trans American Van Service	2,590	270	10.4	14
United Van Lines	117,059	1,443	1.2	4-tie
Von Der Ahe Van Lines	4,136	76	1.8	7
Wheaton Van Lines	26,850	363	1.4	6-tie

Note that Allied Van Lines and Lyon Moving and Storage have significantly better records than some others, such as King and Mayflower.

WHAT THE MOVERS ADMIT: Goofs per 100 Moves

MOVING COMPANY	Over-estimated by 10% or more	Under-estimated by 10% or more	Picked up at least 1 day late	Delivered at least 1 day late	With $50 or more loss or damage claim	With claim for expenses caused by delay	Average no. of days to settle a claim	% claims taking 60 days or more to settle	TOTAL SCORE
Aero Mayflower Transit	33.2	25.4	2.7	9.8	22.8	1.3	33	21.9	150.1
Allied Van Lines	26.5	21.4	6.4	9.5	12.9	1.1	15	8.4	101.2
Allstates Van Lines	16.8	29.5	8.0	9.7	15.7	0.4	41	21.7	142.8
American Red Ball	28.8	24.3	2.6	22.4	20.3	3.3	39	19.9	160.6
Atlas Van Lines	26.1	32.8	3.7	26.1	22.6	2.7	24	15.8	153.8
Bekins Van Lines	35.8	23.8	3.5	17.7	18.2	3.4	23	9.8	135.2
Burnham Van Service	35.5	24.9	0.5	21.0	20.5	2.4	14	0.5	119.3
Engel Van Lines	13.5	18.1	0.8	15.7	9.3	1.5	40	34.5	133.4
Fogarty Van Lines	26.9	24.6	2.0	5.3	27.6	0.3	31	14.5	132.2
Global Van Lines	18.7	14.5	1.1	24.4	10.5	1.9	29	12.8	112.9
Ivory Van Lines	29.9	21.9	3.3	9.4	18.1	1.1	13	8.2	104.9
King Van Lines	16.1	17.9	10.8	27.7	16.2	0.8	55	43.4	187.9
Lyon Moving & Storage	20.7	20.4	1.1	12.7	18.5	0.6	27	6.4	107.4
National Van Lines	26.0	31.5	2.0	19.3	22.8	4.8	51	31.4	188.8
North American Van Lines	27.2	18.2	6.1	10.5	20.8	2.1	24	12.9	121.8
Pan American Van Lines	29.0	23.0	2.3	10.5	14.0	0.2	23	6.0	108.0
Republic Van Lines	20.5	20.4	3.4	14.8	20.8	3.7	39	15.4	138.0
Smyth Van Lines	24.4	26.7	3.3	15.7	17.5	2.0	106	69.0	264.6
United Van Lines	25.6	21.4	4.5	15.6	15.0	1.4	21	9.0	113.5
Wheaton Van Lines	32.7	16.7	1.2	9.6	13.1	2.6	44	33.0	152.9

Source: Interstate Commerce Commission, 1979

If the company you are considering is not on this list, you can get a record of its performance by calling the ICC office closest to you:

Washington, D.C.
(Headquarters)—
   Toll-free no.   800-424-9312
Miami, FL (Calls placed
   within FL)—
   Toll-free no.   800-432-4537
Miami, FL (Calls placed outside FL)   305-350-5551
Boston, MA   617-223-2372
Philadelphia, PA   215-597-4460
Atlanta, GA   404-881-4371
Chicago, IL   312-353-6185
Ft. Worth, TX   817-334-2794
San Francisco, CA   415-556-1392
New York City, NY   212-264-1072
Los Angeles, CA   213-688-4006

PACKING TO MOVE

You can do the packing or you can pay the movers to do it. Movers charge about $3 to pack a carton of books—$12 to pack a carton of dishes. They also charge for the carton itself ($1 for the book carton, $8 for a big mattress carton).

If you want to save by doing the packing yourself, the movers will sell you boxes. However, you can buy much cheaper boxes on your own (look under "Boxes" in the Yellow Pages).

Warnings: (1) Movers are generally better at packing than you are. (2) If what you pack breaks during the move, the mover is not responsible. If a box is too heavy (i.e., you've filled it completely with books), the movers may refuse to move it.

I suggest you pack the soft, nonbreakable items yourself, and leave the fragile stuff to the movers.

When the movers do the packing, keep an eye on them to prevent "balloon packing." That's when they fill a box halfway, seal it up, and charge you for a full box.

You'll probably want to do the *un*packing yourself, so you can take time putting things away. Fragile things should be unpacked immediately. (Mark the box FRAGILE so you can find it and see if there's any damage, BEFORE you sign the inventory.)

STORAGE

Companies tend to call themselves ABC "Moving *and* Storage," but storage is a different and scarier ball game. Moving is licensed and regulated by the ICC. Storage is not. There are plenty of horror stories about moving, but the storage stories are worse. Example:

Patricia Martin was going to Europe for two years, so she called three companies for storage estimates. The lowest estimate was $4,000. "Okay," she told that company, "you take the stuff." Then, she went off to work. The next day, the storage company called, "Patricia, I'm afraid you're furniture was a little heavier than we thought. The bill will be $9,000." "Outrageous," she said. "You gave me a $4,000 estimate; you're stuck with that." And she went off to Europe. The storage company then sold her furniture to pay her bill. When she returned from Europe, most of her furniture was gone. There was nothing, legally, she could do about it.

It's called low-balling. The company gives you a low estimate, then jacks up the bill once they've got your furniture. At that point, you're stuck. If you refuse to pay your bill, they can legally sell your possessions.

All you can do is call the Better Business Bureau and check the company's reputation BEFORE you store. That's not foolproof, but it's all you've got.

In the Supermarket

Normally, when I go around with a camera crew, people notice and make a fuss. "What are you filming?" they ask, "Aren't you what's-his-name from Channel 2?" Not so in supermarkets. We're there with two powerful lights and 3 burly technicians holding camera gear and people walk right into us. Only when light hits them do they look up and say "Huh," and get out of the way.

I think this happens because people go into a trance in supermarkets. We stare at those thousands of different identical products and something goes fssst in the brain. We can't deal with making so many decisions, so we walk around like zombies. I think this is what makes obnoxious TV ads successful. We hate Mr. Whipple so much, his image cuts through the trance and we buy Charmin bathroom tissue.

Vance Packard reports some scientific support for this theory. A researcher once used hidden cameras to note how often people blink in supermarkets. Apparently when we're excited, we blink more. The researcher thought the excitement of being able to choose between so many wonderful products would make supermarket shoppers blink more. To his surprise, he found supermarket customers blinking not faster, but much slower than normal. He decided they were in some kind of light trance.

Supermarkets take advantage of our trance by putting expensive items at eye level, while hiding bargains on top and bottom shelves. They fill end-of-the-aisle bins with high mark-up items because they know most of us assume (incorrectly) that whatever is in those bins must be on sale. They sometimes raise prices at the beginning of the month, because that's when social security and welfare checks come out. Food packagers have their own sets of tricks. If you're well informed about food, you'll save money by not falling for them.

But first, let's talk about health.

NUTRITION AND HEALTH

So many products are labeled "health foods" you'd think we'd live forever. On the other hand, there are so many scare stories about cancer-causing ingredients, cholesterol, and junk foods, it's amazing we're still alive at all.

"Health" claims are pretty meaningless. Any food manufacturer can call a food "health food." There are no regulations forbidding it. The same is true of "natural" food. Some "natural" food has artificial ingredients. When I visit "health" food stores, I find mostly weird foods (Tiger's milk, "natural" vitamin pills) that nutritionists tell me are no more healthful than ordinary food. I also find food in the health food stores costs twice as much as similar food sold in supermarkets. Health stores do sell "organic" food, and if it was indeed grown without exposure to chemical fertilizers and pesticides, it might be better for us. However, far more "organic" food is sold than grown.

Many health food store products are not particularly healthful at all. The protein powders these stores sell are unnecessary to most people and the liquid-protein diets can be harmful. Some health food stores advocate replacing sugar with "raw honey." True, refined sugar isn't great for you because it provides fattening calories without any nutrients. But "raw honey" is just honey with a minor amount of vitamins included; and honey, too, is empty calories.

I think it makes more sense to shop in ordinary supermarkets and simply pay attention to some basic principles of nutrition. Eat something from all four food groups; avoid nitrites, saccharine, excessive additives, empty calories and salt; eat some fiber; eat fresh foods whenever possible, and cook them in a way that retains their nutrients.

The four food groups are (1) meat, fish, nuts, beans (the

protein group); (2) breads and cereals; (3) dairy products; (4) vegetables and fruits (green stuff). If you get some of these every day, you're getting a balanced diet. If you skip a group one day, you can catch up the next day.

I think it's sensible to worry a little about nitrites, saccharine, additives and empty calories, but only a little. I eat them, but I try to eat less of them. It hasn't been conclusively proven that any of these things are harmful, but why take chances?

Nitrites and saccharine have been linked to cancer in animals. But keep things in perspective. An American Cancer Society spokesman says you are far more likely to get cancer breathing cigarette smoke than eating bacon and drinking diet soda every day. You get *nitrites* in processed meats (bacon, hot dogs, bologna, etc.), and *saccharine* in nearly all diet foods. I'd avoid nitrites, but if you are obese, it's better to eat saccharine than sugar.

It's impossible to avoid all additives, because they are now in almost every food, but if you read the labels, you can at least avoid buying products that are chock-full of additives. If a company puts extra chemicals into a food, it must say so on the ingredient label.

MONEY-SAVING IDEAS

Let's start with *when* to shop. As I said, the beginning of the month is to be avoided because some stores raise prices then. The best time to shop is Tuesday or Wednesday, because that's when supermarkets run most of their specials. If you follow the newspaper ads and stock up on midweek sale items you can save a significant amount of money. Even without the price differences, it is better to shop on Tuesdays and Wednesdays because the stores are least crowded then.

The best way to save money in the supermarket is to diligently clip and save coupons. I'm far too lazy to do this, so I don't have real expertise on it. A good guide is Refundle Bundle, P.O. Box 141, Centuck Station, Yonkers, New York 10710. For $9 a year you'll receive a monthly newsletter and a refunding manual. Another good guide is the *National Supermarket Shopper*. It tells you where you can send boxtops for refunds, lists addresses of coupon-swapping clubs, and gives numerous tips on how to get more money for your coupons. Subscriptions cost $15. Mail checks to Circulation Department, Supermarket Shopper, Box 1149, Great Neck, New York 11023.

Understanding the manufacturers' packaging tricks will save you money. Sometimes you pay less for the very same food just because it comes in a different package. Examples of this are store-brand and "no-brand" foods:

NO-BRAND FOOD

It's the stuff in the plain white boxes. It costs about one-third less. It's not just food; cleaning and paper products are sold this way too. Are they as good as the brand-name stuff? Yes and No. I've run several tests with no-frill products, and the results were ambiguous. Some people couldn't tell the difference; most people preferred the brand names; some people preferred the no-brand products.

No-brand products are lower "grade." But the government often grades food according to how they *look,* not how they *taste,* or how *nutritious* they are. No-frills peas may be a little older, but they're just as healthful. No-frills fruits are probably more healthful than regular fruits; they're packed in less sugary syrup (they're also more likely to be in broken pieces). No-brand detergent is often brand-name detergent, without the fancy colors and smells.

The moral: Try it. It's much cheaper. Tests show most people like *some* of the no-brand products better.

STORE BRANDS

Most supermarkets also sell their own "house" or "store" brands.

Store brands usually cost somewhere in between brand-name and no-brand food. If the store brand is named after the supermarket, it's probably just as good as a brand-name product. If it goes by some other name, it's probably a lower "grade" similar to a no-brand type. A&P, for example, calls its high-grade store brands "A&P Peas," "A&P Ice Cream," etc. The store brands it is less proud of it calls "Ann Page Peas," "Ann Page Ice Cream."

A FEW OTHER TIPS

A *bad buy:* drinks in cans. Iced tea in a can, for example, costs 33¢ at my supermarket. You can make your own tea from tea bags for 9¢. Fruit drinks are usually lots of water with very little fruit. Soft drinks are a terrible buy. You're paying 33¢ a can for carbonated sugar water.

When buying frozen food, watch out for packages with ice crystals on them. That means the package has been thawed and then refrozen. It's probably safe, but it might taste bad. Also, you may have noticed supermarket freezer compartments have a line that runs a few inches from the top. Anything below that line is cold enough to stay frozen. Above the line, who knows?

We know that convenience foods usually cost more. For example, the U.S. Agriculture Department says frozen shrimp Newburg costs $1.13 per serving, yet you can make it yourself for 66¢. However, don't assume you always save by doing it yourself. Some convenience foods actually cost less. The Agriculture Department says it costs 35¢ per serving to make fish cakes at home, but you can buy them frozen for 22¢ (taste is another matter). Frozen orange juice is cheaper than bottled, and much cheaper than buying oranges and squeezing them yourself. Frozen french fries cost 7¢ per serving. Buying the potatoes and making the fries yourself costs 10¢. Canned peas and corn are cheaper than fresh. Instant coffee is cheaper than regular.

When buying eggs, consider grade B. They're just as nutritious as Grade A or AA and they taste the same. The only difference: The yolks don't stand up as high in the pan. But unless you're poaching or frying them, who cares?

Also, eggs stay fresher longer if you store them pointed end *down.*

MEAT

They rip you off when they cut it. The supermarkets say, "It's fair, we're just charging for labor." Maybe, but then they must pay their butchers $500.00 per hour. You're better off buying a big piece and cutting it yourself. Examples: At my supermarket, boneless chuck costs $2.09 per pound, top chuck costs $1.69. Yet plain chuck steak costs only $1.09 per pound, and when you cut it in half you get top chuck and boneless chuck. It's even more impressive with the expensive cuts. Filet costs $6.69. Shell steak costs $4.29. Yet you get both filet and shell if you cut a porterhouse steak in half. Porterhouse costs $3.29. A cookbook which gives detailed instructions on how to cut down larger cuts of meat can pay for itself in less than a month.

If you can't afford beef, don't worry about it. Nutritionists say Americans eat much more beef than necessary. Chicken and turkey are cheaper and more healthful. Even without meat, you can give your family all the protein they need by feeding them milk, cheese, beans, eggs, or peanut butter; $2.00 worth of sirloin gives you no more protein than 70¢ worth of red beans, 50¢ worth of eggs, or 40¢ worth of peanut butter.

You've seen ads promoting "meat in bulk." SAVE! BUY FROM US AT WHOLESALE PRICES. BUY 100 POUNDS AND STORE IN YOUR FREEZER. Watch out. In New York there's a company called Custom Meats. They have fifteen stores and run full-color ads in the newspapers promoting a package of T-bone, chuck, sirloin, and porterhouse steak for a wonderful 99¢ a pound. I bought 92 pounds worth. Then I took it to a meat expert and had him reweigh it.

Harold Sherman, Meat Specialist, N.Y.C. Dept. of Consumer Affairs:
    "Seventy-six pounds."
Stossel: "Seventy-six?"
Harold Sherman: "That's with the paper."
Stossel: "So we were shortchanged fifteen pounds of meat."
Harold Sherman: "Immediately—yes."
Stossel (to audience): That's not necessarily a gyp. Custom Meats claims the weight drops because they trim away bone and fat, and just leave the best stuff. Still, that made the price we paid now $1.20 per pound.

Harold Sherman: "And you even paid $1.20 for two and a half pounds of paper."

Stossel (to audience): Then we examined the supposedly trimmed meat.

Harold Sherman: "This is untrimmed."

Stossel: "What does that mean?"

Harold Sherman: "That means a supermarket would never sell it this way. They would cut this piece of fat out completely. You'll never buy it in a supermarket with this fat in it."

Stossel: "So not only did we pay more, but we paid for fat?"

Harold Sherman: "Right."

Stossel: "The advertisements say this is prime meat. Is this prime meat?"

Harold Sherman: "No—in my estimation it's definitely not prime meat."

Stossel (to audience): Sherman said some packages were mislabeled. What they called steak was really stew meat.

Harold Sherman: ". . . definitely not steak."

Stossel: "They're selling stew meat for steak?"

Harold Sherman: "For steak. And when it comes to stew meat, there's more bone—very little stew meat. And they didn't even have the decency to clean off the bone dust when they sold it. Nowhere— in no supermarket will you find a piece of meat put out in this condition—with the bone dust still on it."

Stossel: "How can these people get away with doing that?"

Harold Sherman: "They are not doing anything illegal. Maybe immoral or unethical, but it's not illegal."

Elaine Rose Ruderman, Consumer Economist, Cornell University: "You were taken in by an ad. You were hoping that the ad was going to promise you many months of fine eating. And it's not going to."

Stossel: "What is it providing me with?"

Elaine Rose Ruderman: "Well—do you like soup?"

Stossel (to audience): Not at chuck steak prices. I tried to confront Custom Meats with what they'd sold us, but no luck. The owner refuses to be interviewed. "Do you want to talk on camera?" we asked. "Do I want bubonic plague?" he replied.

We went to a Sloan's supermarket and compared Custom Meats' meat with Sloan's. The meat expert said the supermarket meat was better, and averaged 80¢ a pound cheaper.

Moral: If you have a freezer, wait for the supermarket sales. Stock up then.

BREAD

To get value buying bread, don't buy by size; buy by weight. Some bread is puffed up with air. You think you are getting a lot of bread for your money, but in fact you're buying air at bread prices.

A lot of people assume it's nutritionally better to buy dark breads. We tend to believe that white bread has the nutrients processed out, while dark bread still has them inside. Not necessarily true. Dark bread is sometimes simply white bread, dyed dark. There's no definite data on what bread may be better for you, but consider this: Consumers Union bought thirty-three brands of bread and fed them to laboratory rats. Then they weighed and measured to see how much each rat grew or did not grow. The study found it made no difference whether the rats ate dark or white bread. It also made no difference whether the bread was "enriched." The bread companies that I called said the test was ridiculous, since no one eats only bread. Nutritionists I called said if you want a more nutritious bread, buy whole wheat. Whole wheat has more nutrients left in. The word "wheat" alone, or "health food" bread doesn't mean anything.

CANNED FOODS

How fresh is canned food? Is your baby food older than the baby? Some companies now print pull dates on cans. A Hellmann's mayonnaise jar will say in plain English, "Buy before July 10, 1982." Good for Hellmann's. A Campbell's soup can will say "September, 1981." That's the pull date. This is helpful, to a point; 1981 means Campbell's says the soup is good at least until then. You don't know if the soup was packed last year, or perhaps ten years ago. In Campbell's case, the company believes the soups have a shelf life of three years. Different companies have different beliefs about shelf life. Worse, some companies print the dates in code: 7-1-9-3-0-1 on a box of Duncan Hines cake mix means the mix was packed in July, 1977. Knowing the pack date is the most useful; that tells you exactly how old the food is. If you write to the New York State Consumer Protection Board, Empire Street Plaza, Albany, N.Y. 12210, they'll send you a booklet that tells you how to decode the code to get the pack date. Ask for the "Blind Dates" booklet.

Why aren't the pack dates posted in plain English? Food companies worry that if consumers knew the dates, we'd buy only the freshest products (Yes, we probably would). So older products would have to be thrown out. That would cost everybody more. Then why not put the older food on sale (like they do with old bread)? Consumers ought to be able to tell the age of food without having to break a code.

STORING FOOD

If you have a freezer, you probably buy meat on sale and freeze it so you can cook it later. If you're like me, you forget you've frozen it, discover it months later, and wonder whether it's safe to eat. Some guidelines:

The U.S. Agriculture Department says beef will keep for a year if kept frozen at 0°. Most freezers keep food at 0°. Pork will keep for only six months, and chicken for only two months. If kept longer they become dry, though it will still have as much protein and iron as it had the day you threw it into the freezer.

Eventually all meat will spoil, even if it's been frozen. Freezing slows the growth of bacteria, but doesn't stop it altogether. If the meat smells funny, or looks a little green, don't eat it. If you did, it probably wouldn't kill you. You'd certainly get a stomach ache, but it's not so dangerous as the poisoning you can get eating spoiled food from a can.

The *way* you wrap food affects its freshness too. Heavy-duty aluminum foil is the best wrap, because you can mold it tightly around the meat. This eliminates air pockets and keeps the meat from drying out. I suggest *heavy*-duty foil, because thinner foil may get little holes in it. Freezer paper is good, and tears less easily than foil. However, freezer paper doesn't mold as well.

If you're storing food for shorter periods, or just putting things in the refrigerator, there's no need to spend the money for foil or freezer paper. Plastic wrap does the job.

Tip: Plastic wrap will be less annoyingly electric if you *snap* it out of the roll, rather than pulling it out slowly. Storing it in the refrigerator accomplishes the same thing.

Tip: Don't store fruits, tomato sauce, or salty food in aluminum foil. Salt rusts foil. Fruits and tomato sauce eat into it.

Tip: Cottage cheese keeps fresher longer if you store the container upside down. Better put something underneath, however, in case of leaks.

FRUITS AND VEGETABLES

The secret of getting good products is to buy in season. If you buy cherries in September, plums and prunes in May, brussels sprouts in June, you pay more for lousy food (cherries are sweetest in August, plums and prunes peak in July, brussels sprouts are best in November).

Why fight nature? The following chart tells you what to buy when. The numbers represent the percentage of the food available at that time. High numbers come right after harvest, and that's generally when the food is the cheapest, freshest, and tastes the best. Some foods, like apples, store well, so you can buy out of season without problem. Not so with blueberries, peaches, or corn.

FOOD	Jan. %	Feb. %	Mar. %	Apr. %	May %	June %	July %	Aug. %	Sept. %	Oct. %	Nov. %	Dec. %
APPLES	9	9	10	9	8	6	3	4	9	12	10	11
APRICOTS					7	58	29	6				
ARTICHOKES	3	5	11	22	21	10	4	4	4	6	5	5
ASPARAGUS		7	25	34	20	9			1	2	1	
AVOCADOS						GOOD ALL YEAR						
Florida	11	3					5	11	11	17	26	16
BANANAS						GOOD ALL YEAR						
BEANS, SNAP, all				9	10	12	11	10	9	8	7	7
Florida	11	5	6	20	14	17	16	17	15	2	13	14
California		9	14	1	9	11	13	12	10	13	10	2
BEETS	5	5	8	7	7				2	9	7	6
BLUEBERRIES						24	48	24				
BROCCOLI	9	8	12	8	2	8	7	5	7	8	9	11
BRUSSELS SPROUTS	13	12	11	8	4			2	6	14	16	13
CABBAGE	9	8	10	9					8	8	8	8
Florida	16	14	23	20	9	9	7	7	1	2	1	7
Texas	16	14	15	13	15	3	2	1	6	7	8	14
California	10	9	10	9	10	4	7	6	12	15	8	8
New York	10	7	5	2	10	10	8	10	8	7	17	12
North Carolina	1		3	4	1	31	8	8	12	4	15	10
CANTALOUPES												
California					12	19	24	23	17	6	1	
Mexico		2	16	28	44	14	28	32			2	
Texas					18	47	21	11	2			
CARROTS	10	9	10	9	8	8	7	7	8	8	8	8

FOOD	Jan. %	Feb. %	Mar. %	Apr. %	May %	June %	July %	Aug. %	Sept. %	Oct. %	Nov. %	Dec. %
CAULIFLOWER	8	7	9	9	8	7	6	6	8	12	11	9
CELERY	9	8	9	9	8	8	7	7	7	7	11	10
Florida	17	14	18	18	15	7	1				2	7
Michigan							18	29	32	18	2	
CHERRIES, SWEET								6				
CORN, SWEET, all	3	2	4		6	42	46					3
Florida	5	4	5	7	16	18	17	14	7	5	4	6
California				13	26	23	5	18		6	7	
New York					9	30	23	48	10	7	4	
CRANBERRIES									37	25	45	20
CUCUMBERS	6	5	6	9	11	13	12	9	10	8	8	6
Florida	4	1	3	18	26	11	1		7	8	17	10
Mexico	23	22	22	12	3						2	15
California			1	3	11	17	20	16	13	10	6	2
EGGPLANT						GOOD ALL YEAR						
GRAPEFRUIT, all	12	12	13	11	9	6	3	3	4	7	10	10
Florida	12	12	13	13	10	5	2		2		11	10
Texas	19	19	17	11	5					4	10	14
Western	4	5	5	7	12	16	17			2	3	3
GRAPES, table	3	2	4	3	2	6	10	19	10	15	10	7
HONEYDEWS	1	1	2	3	6	15	12	19	19	14	4	2
LEMONS	8	7	8	8	9	10	10	10	21	7	7	8
LETTUCE	7	8	9	9	9	9	9	9	8	8	8	7
Arizona	11	7	11	23	7	1			8	3	8	21
Florida	16	13	21	21	9	1					15	12
LIMES	7	4	6	6	8	11	12	12	10	7	6	9
MANGOS		2	4	6	14	24	24	19	5	1	8	
MUSHROOMS						GOOD ALL YEAR			16	1		
NECTARINES		1			10	19	32	30	11	1		
OKRA	2	3	8	8		14	15	15		8	4	2

PEARS											
Washington, Oregon	7	6	7	6	5	4	4	13	13	1	10	8
California	11	11	10	8	5	2	1	5	16	14	12	12
PEAS, GREEN	1	15	11	11	13	14	11	34	10	14	6	1
PEPPERS												
Florida	13	7	7	8	9	10	8	5	27	19	6	4
California	8	9	11	17	19	10	10	16	3	2	6	12
PINEAPPLES	14	7	11	10	2	6	1	7	21	25	14	12
PLUMS & FRESH PRUNES			1	11	12	13	14	35	4	5	6	1
California	7	7	9	8	8	13	10	8	19	2	8	8
POTATOES, all		1	4	2	7	8	10	10	4	9	4	4
California	9	8	4	8	9	8	1	1	19	9	9	11
Idaho	5	4	12	7	19	26	14	13	9	5	4	11
Maine	12	11	15	13	13	9	10	1	5	1	9	15
North Dakota	16	12	14	16	13	3	1	13	1	3	8	11
Wisconsin	15	13	7	12	5	2		1	3	8	13	15
RHUBARB	12	8	17	22	21	10	2	6	19	13	9	9
SPINACH	8	15	11	10	9	9	6	6	1	1	1	1
SQUASH							**GOOD ALL YEAR**		7	8	8	8
STRAWBERRIES, all	2	3	8	19	29	16	9	5	4	2	1	2
California			5	19	33	17	11	6	5	5	1	
SWEET POTATOES	9	8	9	8	4	3	2	5	9	9	19	13
TANGERINES	19	11	9	5	1					11	20	28
TOMATOES, all	7	6	8	9	11	10	11	9	7	6	7	7
California	1					6	18	16	17	8	13	6
Florida	13	8	13	23	15	8					8	16
Mexico	12	17	21	21	17	6	1			1	2	4
Ohio			7	7	17	24	25	10	4	5	5	2
WATERMELONS		1	3	12	28	29	18	6	6	1		

Source: United Fresh Fruit and Vegetable Association, Alexandria, Virginia

The chart represents averages, of course. Weird weather will mess things up.

Now that you know *when*, here's specific advice about some of the products:

Apples. "Delicious" apples are the sweetest. It doesn't matter if they're red or yellow.

Broccoli. It should be all green. If there are yellow traces, that means it's old, and will be tough and chewy.

Bananas. Yes, contrary to the old ads, you can store them in the refrigerator. Sure, they'll turn black, but only on the outside. The insides turn black quicker if they're not in the refrigerator.

Beans. Pick them by feel. One dealer says his best bean grader is a blind man. A good bean feels smooth and silky.

Cantaloupe. The rougher the skin, the sweeter the fruit. To test for ripeness, press the end to see if it's soft. No, not the end that looks like a belly button. That's where the stem was attached—it's always soft. To test for ripeness, press the other end.

Eggplant. Pick the lighter ones. They have fewer seeds.

Mushrooms. The good ones feel smooth and dry, not slimy or sticky.

Papaya. This is a good substitute for melon during the winter. An unripe papaya will be light green. Keep it out of the refrigerator a few days. When it turns light yellow, it's ripe.

How do you ripen fruit?

I was taught to put it on the windowsill. That's ridiculous. The sun simply dries the fruit out. Just as I was getting used to shriveled fruit, I learned the right way: put the fruit in a grocery or plastic bag. Fruits release ethylene gas as they ripen; containing the gas in the bag speeds the process. Once it's ripe, refrigerating it helps it keep.

BABY FOOD

They finally took the sugar and salt out of baby foods. Now the danger is that you'll put it back in. If you taste your baby's food, you'll find it bland. Resist the temptation to spice it. Your baby doesn't find it bland; only you do.

A study done in an orphanage found that some children never given sugar never developed a sweet tooth. Millions of adults today must diet, and hate it, only because they ate sugar when they were babies.

Many adults have high blood pressure becuase they eat too much salt. If they never developed a taste for it as babies . . .

Now that baby-food makers have taken the chemicals out of baby food, don't spoil it for your children by spicing their food.

DIET FOODS

Diet foods tend to cost more. Sometimes it's worth it. If manufacturers have taken the time to reformulate a food so it has less sugar or fat, they deserve extra money to cover their costs. If you can stand the taste, buy it.

Often diet food is not worth the money. In many instances, it's just a gimmick designed to trick you into paying more for less food.

Some con games: Diet bread is often ordinary bread, sliced thinner. Look for the calories *per ounce.*

Diet margarine is often ordinary margarine with water added. Look at the ingredient label. If water is listed before other ingredients, you're simply paying margarine prices for water.

Your supermarket probably has a big display promoting "Dietetic Foods." Once I stopped in front of such a display and asked shoppers about it.

Stossel: "What does that sign 'dietetic' mean?"

Woman #1 in supermarket: "Less calories, and good for anyone who wants to watch their diet."

Woman #2 in supermarket: "Less calories, it has less calories. I use it. I'm on a diet."

Man in supermarket: "It has special sugars in it that don't put on fat."

That's logical, but unfortunately, wrong. Dietetic foods are often just as fattening as other foods. Sometimes they are even more fattening. They almost always *cost* more. Dietetic means:

for people with diabetes or people on special diets. Dietetic food sometimes contains calorie-free saccharine but it usually substitutes sorbitol for regular sugar. Sorbitol is slower acting sugar. It doesn't send your blood sugar over the roller coaster as regular sugar does. This is great for diabetics, but useless for dieters. Sorbitol is just as fattening as regular sugar. If you're on a diet you want "diet" food, not "dietetic" food.

SOAPS

Do you buy because of the soap or the box? In *Hidden Persuaders,* Vance Packard tells of researchers who gave consumers three detergents and requested that they try them all out and then report which was best for delicate clothing. The consumers thought they'd been given three different types of detergent. Actually only the boxes were different; the detergents were identical.

The design for one was predominantly yellow. Yellow was used because some researchers were convinced that yellow was the best color for store shelves because it has very strong visual impact. Another box was predominantly blue; the third box was blue with splashes of yellow.

In their reports the consumers stated that the detergent in the brilliant yellow box was too strong; it even allegedly ruined their clothes in some cases. As for the detergent in the blue box, the testers complained that it left their clothes dirty looking. The third box overwhelmingly received favorable responses. The testers used such words as "fine" and "wonderful" in describing the effect the detergent in that box had on their clothes.

What should *you* use to wash clothes?

It seemed easier when you just took the clothes to the river and smashed them against a rock. Today we've got pre-soaks, fabric softeners, bleach, phosphates, non-phosphates. I guess we don't think we're clean enough. Here's how you can get clean for less money.

Although it doesn't seem logical, tests have shown that cold-water washing gets clothes just about as clean as hot water. Using cold water saves you fuel money (it may cost you $50 a year to heat the water) and makes your clothes last longer (hot water is harder on fabrics). Hot water will kill more bacteria, so think about that if there's a sick person in the house. But most bacteria die as the clothes dry anyway.

I don't think it matters which brand of detergent you use, but don't use more detergent than the machine instructions recommend; it can damage the machine. In fact you can probably get away with using less than the detergent box recommends; the soap maker has an incentive to tell you to use *too* much. He makes money that way.

A lot of these new wonder products have little drawbacks the manufacturers don't like to tell you about. For example, fabric softeners do soften clothes and eliminate static electricity. However, they also make fabrics slightly less absorbent. That's a problem if they happen to be towels or diapers. Also, although some manufacturers claim fabric softeners whiten clothes, *Consumer Reports* claims fabric softeners actually make clothes look yellow and dingy.

Bleach makes clothes look whiter. But it also damages fibers slightly. Clothes will last longer if you don't need to bleach. Never use extra bleach; the extra amount damages the garments without making them any whiter. Above all, don't mix bleach with ammonia cleaners. Combining them makes chlorine gas, which is deadly.

Tip: To make bars of soap last longer, unwrap them right after you buy them. When soap has been exposed to air during storage, it dissolves more slowly.

BUYING WATER

If you buy water, I assume you are (1) terrified that tap water will poison you, or (2) you like the taste of bottled water.

1. I think most tap water is perfectly safe. It's tested constantly. Lab analyses I've done have found tap water to be as clean as (in some cases cleaner than) bottled water. Bottled spring water, from underground, is clean to start with. But it can get contaminated during transportation and bottling.

If you are concerned about your local tap water, you may be

tempted to buy one of those home water filters. Usually you screw them on to the tap. Unfortunately most filters don't do what people think they do. They don't remove chlorine, and are not very effective against bacteria. The better filters cost more, at least $50 to $100, and usually fit under the sink.

2. If you really prefer the taste of bottled water, buy it. But if you're getting it because your family *says* they like it, try a test. Give them several types of bottled water and tap water in unmarked glasses. I bet they can't tell the difference between tap and the uncarbonated bottled waters. And I bet they like the cheap bottled water as well as the expensive. We ran our own taste test at WCBS and the results were as follows (most liked, first):

1. Club soda
2. Tap water (Nobody would believe it when we told them they were praising tap water.)
3. Foodtown
4. Deer Park
5. Great Bear
6. Perrier
7. Vichy

The big sellers didn't do very well. Most people buy them because they're manipulated by the advertising. The ads don't lie, but sometimes they are misleading. With Poland Spring Water, the water comes from Maine, but the carbonation comes out of a mine in Colorado. And they call it "natural mineral water." Schweppes Sparkling Mineral Water with its "Schweppervescence" turns out to be Los Angeles tap water with artificial carbonation and salt added.

LIQUOR

Snob appeal, not taste, sells the expensive brands. Some distillers reluctantly raised their prices and were delighted to find that increased sales.

Take vodka. You might as well save $4 and buy the cheapest. Nobody can tell the difference. As defined by Federal law, vodka has to be nothing but tasteless grain alcohol diluted with water. If you must impress your guests, buy the cheap and pour it into an expensive bottle.

Connoisseurs can tell the difference between different brands of gin, bourbon, Scotch, and beer. Most of us are not connoisseurs. In fact some people who swear they can taste the difference cannot. I've blindfolded a number of people who claimed to be able to recognize their favorite brands of beer. Almost none could.

Stossel: "Which do you like?"

Man in bar: "Glass 3 was good, 2 was okay, glass 1 was bleccch. I think 3 was Budweiser."

Stossel: "Budweiser is your favorite brand?"

Man in bar: "Yeah."

Stossel: "Glass number 1 was Budweiser."

Man in bar: "Shit."

Another man in bar: "I liked glass 1; 2 didn't have any taste."

Stossel: "Do you like Budweiser?"

Man: "I hate Budweiser."

Stossel: "Number 1 was Budweiser."

Man: "Gimme a break."

Stossel: "No, really, number 1 is Budweiser."

Man: "Gimme a break."

Some long-time beer drinkers couldn't even tell beer from ale.

Two final tips: Watch out for the new metric sizes. Liquor companies are using them to sneak in price increases. The new 1¾-liter size looks like the old half gallon, and often costs the same, but it holds 4.8 ounces less liquor. In addition, some companies are keeping their prices the same, but lowering the proof.

You can check this by reading the label. The label has to list the proof.

Health, Cosmetics and Drugs

People often ask me: "What's the worst ripoff you've covered?" I can never pick a single topic, so I always answer that the biggest ripoff *area* is cosmetics and drugs. Nowhere else do people get so much bull and so little value for their money. Misleading commercials offer us a drug for every medical problem. In truth, many of these drugs are useless, and a few are harmful. Cheaper remedies are ignored because drug companies don't make a profit on them. This chapter will tell you what the drug companies don't want you to know.

LOSING WEIGHT

I put this first because it seems to be on everybody's mind. Most of the stuff they sell to help us lose weight doesn't work. A few things do work, however. Let's sort them out.

What doesn't work: Most of the pills advertised in the backs of magazines. All of the creams and lotions you smear on. The squeeze-your-fat away devices. The cellulite-removing devices. All the products that "burn fat." The machines in the health spas that shake, vibrate and rub you.

I've sent away for the pills. They are usually just vitamin pills, or "swell-up" pills. Swell-up pills absorb moisture and swell up when they get into your stomach; that's supposed to make you feel full. It's a logical concept, but an FDA panel says there's no evidence that swell-up pills help people lose weight. Vitamins don't work simply because vitamins have nothing to do with losing or gaining weight.

The creams and lotions won't hurt you. Many are simply moisturizers. None is of any help in removing fat or pounds. I get a kick out of the squeeze-em devices. I've gone to a couple of spas that use them. They wrap you tightly in ace bandages or tape and then leave you in a hot room for an hour. It's the same principle that's behind the "trimming belts." "sauna corsets," and other devices sold by mail order. ("Lose inches while you sleep!") The idea is to squeeze fat out of you (as you sweat the fat will supposedly "melt away," particularly from the places being squeezed most tightly). It doesn't work. What's being squeezed out is water, not fat. You *will* find yourself thinner if you measure yourself immediately afterward. But since the loss is water, the inches come right back as soon as you drink something.

It's easy to believe that there are different kinds of fat, in need of different treatments. For instance, you always hear about "cellulite" in those "get slim" ads. It looks different, after all, and even thin people often have "cellulite" bulges on their thighs. Yet, every medical expert we consulted says it just isn't so. There is no such thing as cellulite. Fat is fat is fat. And the only way to get rid of it is to diet. The reason fat stays on some parts of your body after you've lost weight elsewhere is genetic. Your genes have chosen to distribute your fat in those places. If you keep dieting, those parts will eventually get thinner too.

"Burning fat" is the big pitch in the newspaper ads today. It seems logical that fat would "burn" if you just had the right pill to start the fire. Sorry, none of the "burn fat" products do anything useful. Most are just vitamin pills. It's funny that so many newspapers that try to do a good job on the editorial side accept ads for obviously phony diet aids. Anything for money, I guess.

The machines in the health spas that shake and pound you do absolutely no good. For a machine to help you lose weight, you have to do the straining yourself. Jiggling the fat in one area doesn't make any of it go away.

What does work: Eating less. Exercising more. Boring, I know. There are some pills that may help you eat less. They come in two categories. I don't recommend either, but they are legal and they do help some people to diet.

Category 1: amphetamines. Some people call them "diet pills." The kids who sell them on street corners call them greenies, uppers and speed. The kids take them to get high. Baseball pitchers used to take them before games. They didn't pitch any better, but they thought they did ("Hey coach, whaddaya takin' me out for?"). Amphetamines are big-time prescription drugs. They are addictive, and people occasionally kill themselves misusing them. Doctors sometimes will prescribe amphetamines to help fat patients diet. Amphetamines make you feel energetic and somehow also diminish your interest in eating. They also reduce your interest in sleeping, so sometimes "diet pill" patients get hooked on sleeping pills too. Up and down, up and down.

Category 2: benzocaine and phenylpropanolamine. These are milder drugs. Drugstores sell them. You don't need a prescription. Some brand names are:

PHENYLPROPANOLAMINE PRODUCTS
Appedrine*
Ayds Appetite Suppressant Capsules*
Coffee, Tea & A New Me
Control
Dexatrim*
Hungrex-Plus*
Permathene-12*
Power Slim
Prolamine*
Super-Odrinex Tablets*
Vita-Slim

BENZOCAINE PRODUCTS
Ayds Appetite Suppressant Candy
Slim-Line Candy
Slim-Line Chewing Gum

There are other brands available. If a diet product contains benzocaine or phenylpropanolamine it will say so on the label. Some studies found that phenylpropanolamine reduced people's appetites without the harmful side effects of amphetamines. But be careful. The products with an asterisk after them will probably give you a speedy effect because they are full of caffeine. The companies say they put caffeine in because dieting is depressing and caffeine perks you up. I think they put it in because the "caffeine high" will encourage people to buy more pills.

Benzocaine comes in candy form. You suck on the candy and the benzocaine deadens your taste buds. Food doesn't taste as good, and supposedly, you eat less.

There is no solid proof that either of these drugs will help you lose weight. They seem to help some people but not others. In addition, although the FDA review panel called both drugs "safe and effective," there are safety questions about phenylpropanolamine. An article in the highly respected medical journal *Lancet* says taking even a single capsule of a phenylpropanolamine drug may cause "potentially dangerous rises in blood pressure." You should definitely *not* take phenylpropanolamine if you have high blood pressure. You should also not take it if you have diabetes, heart disease, thyroid disease, or if you're being treated for depression. If the drug causes nervousness, dizziness, or sleeplessness, you should stop taking it at once.

One last thought about losing weight. Many people think that to take fat off your stomach, you should do situps and stomach exercises. To take fat from your thighs, do thigh exercises, and so on. It seems logical, but it doesn't work. The only way to take fat off one specific place is to cut it out surgically. When you exercise, you burn fat all over your body, not just in the areas you're exercising. This was discovered by studying tennis players, who have just as much fat in their playing arm as their other arm. Of course, you do build *muscle* by exercising specific areas, so although doing situps won't remove stomach fat, the tighter muscles will make your stomach look better.

HEALTH SPAS

They really are a good deal *if you use them*. Most people don't. Most people get all psyched up at their trial visit, pay $400 for a year's membership, and then gradually lose interest. A government report found most spa members *never* use the spa after three months. Spas are a good deal for regular users because their memberships are subsidized by the dropouts.

Think about the dropout percentage when they give you the sales pitch. And the pitch is often hard-sell. I sent a researcher to a Jack LaLanne spa during a snowstorm. They offered her a "today only" special "snowy-day price." Upon investigation, the "special" price turned out to be more than the regular price.

Once you've paid, you're stuck. In most states, you cannot get out of your membership contract even if you get sick, your work hours change, or the spa turns sleazy. Many spas don't live up to their advertisements, so never sign up by phone, or for a spa that's "opening next month." I'd always demand a "trial day" visit. Good spas offer them. Try the spa out during the hours you plan to use it. The pool may be empty in the morning, but packed when you want to use it after work.

Of the machines at the spas, the ones that vibrate and jiggle your fat do absolutely no good. The only machines that help you lose weight or tone up are ones that require *you* to do the straining. Jiggling the fat on your thighs won't make any of it go away. The spas offer these useless machines because customers *think* they help. They don't.

COLDS AND COLD MEDICINES

"Give your cold to Contac," says the ad. A more accurate ad would say: "Keep your cold . . . give your money to Contac." Neither Contac nor any other cold medicine will cure a cold or even shorten its duration. Thousands of people believe they will, and thereby help drug companies make millions.

Two ingredients in cold medicines will at least relieve cold *symptoms:* (1) Aspirin relieves muscle aches, sore throats, headache, and other pains. Take it with a full glass of water. More on aspirin on page 114; (2) A nasal decongestant helps dry up a runny nose. Best to take it in spray (rather than pill) form. Afrin, Dristan, Duration, and Neo-Synephrine are all good. Be careful not to overuse the sprays. Overuse can rebound—you end up with *more* congestion. I know a man who was "addicted" to sprays. He had a constant runny nose. He'd spray, get temporary relief, and in a few hours his nose would be clogged again. Then he'd spray again. This went on for a year. Finally a doctor told him about rebound. He stopped using the spray and his nose stopped running.

In the latter stage of a cold, when your nose is more "stuffed up" than runny, it's better to loosen the mucous than to dry it out with a decongestant. Using a vaporizer and drinking lots of liquids helps.

Most cold tablets contain aspirin and a decongestant, but the well-known brands charge huge markups. Plain aspirin is cheaper and just as good. Plain nasal sprays are cheaper and work better than the decongestants in the cold pills.

Contac, Dristan, and the other best sellers contain chemicals besides aspirin and a decongestant. It gives the company the opportunity to advertise: "101 ingredients!" However, experts we consulted say the "other ingredients" in Contac, Dristan, etc., will not affect your cold, nor relieve its symptoms.

If you go to a doctor when you have a cold, the physician may prescribe antibiotics. These are very useful—but only for the doctor, not you. Antibiotics kill bacteria. Colds, however, are caused by viruses, not bacteria. Antibiotics have no effect on viruses at all. Okay, by taking an antibiotic you do reduce the chance of secondary infections (like bronchitis), but it's better *not* to take the antibiotics until you already have the infection. Taking antibiotics frequently is dangerous because your body eventually becomes resistant or even allergic to that antibiotic. Then someday, when you really need the medication, you won't be able to take it or it won't help you. Why do doctors prescribe antibiotics to patients with colds? Because the patients are paying for office visits and feel they damn well better get something tangible for the money. If the doctor said, "You have a cold. We don't know how to cure it. It will go away in seven to twelve days. Take aspirin and nasal spray. $25 please," you'd feel cheated. If the physician prescribes an important-sounding drug like tetracycline, you feel you've gotten your money's worth. You haven't.

There's other confusion about colds. First, a cold has nothing to do with the *temperature* cold. That's a myth. Your mother was misinformed when she yelled: "Don't get chilled. You'll catch cold." You can get chilled, wet your feet, roll around in the snow, whatever, without increasing the chance you'll catch a cold. Cold is a virus you get from people who have colds, not from being *cold*. The reason we have more colds in winter is that the cold air drives us indoors, where we spend more time breathing one another's viruses.

If you don't want to pass your cold on to someone else, stay away from people during the first three days; that's when you are most contagious (you are also very contagious one day before the first symptoms arrive, but of course, you don't know when that is).

COUGHS

Cough medicine is another example of a drug more helpful to drug companies than sick people. First of all, coughing is sometimes your body's way of trying to get well. That phlegm you're coughing up is something your body needs to expel. You don't want to suppress that kind of cough. To relieve the throat irritation without suppressing the useful cough, suck on a few hard candies. "Medicated" lozenges do the same thing for twice the price and no additional benefit. *The Medical Letter*, which advises doctors on drug performance, suggests you stick with simple candy drops. Breathing the humid air from a steam or cold-mist vaporizer ($10 to $20) will also relieve the discomfort caused by coughs. *The Medical Letter* says breathing steam is better than taking cough drugs.

If you do insist on a cough syrup, I suggest you get a doctor to prescribe one rather than buying a bottle off the drugstore shelf. The drugstore types usually contain decongestants, of which *The Medical Letter* says: "There is no evidence that these drugs help relieve coughs." Sometimes they contain antihistamines, which "can have an unpleasant drying effect on the respiratory mucosa." A prescription will get you a more effective drug. It will contain an ingredient like codeine, which deadens the cough reflex by deadening the nervous system.

Don't be fooled by ads for "night time" cough remedies. True, coughs are often most bothersome at night; but the "night" medicines are usually the same cough formulas with anti-histamines or alcohol (Nyquil is 50 proof) added to make you drowsy. If you want that effect, vodka is cheaper.

Will Vitamin C cure your cold? I doubt it. I take 2,000 mg a day when I feel a cold coming on *just in case*. But there's no reliable evidence that Vitamin C works. The good studies (where they give a zillion people Vitamin C, and another zillion a placebo and then compare the results) have been inconclusive. In any case, I don't recommend taking massive doses of Vitamin C *every day*. There's no *proof* that so much Vitamin C is harmful, but some scientists believe it might hurt your kidneys. It's a bad idea to take *massive* doses of anything.

SORE THROATS

Sore throats are tough to treat. Some are caused by cold viruses; no drug yet discovered will help viruses go away. Other sore throats are caused by germs; in those cases antibiotics will help. Strep throat, for example, must be treated with antibiotics or it might eventually cause heart or kidney damage. Yet, you don't want to take antibiotics "just in case" because they can be harmful. A good rule of thumb: If a sore throat persists three days, go to a doctor.

To relieve the pain, doctors suggest gargling with warm salt water. Gargling with mouthwashes will also help relieve the pain but, contrary to what the ads used to say, mouthwash will not prevent sore throats or speed their departure. The government got Listerine to run ads saying: "Listerine will *not* prevent colds or sore throats." Aspergum is another genius marketing ploy. By putting aspirin in gum, the company leaves the impression that gradually swallowing the aspirin will soothe the sore throat. It's a logical thought, but not true. It appears aspirin doesn't kill pain by touching something; it works through the bloodstream. Aspergum's manufacturer paid for a study which the company claims shows aspirin *can* relieve pain by directly touching the throat. But every independent aspirin expert we consulted said that's highly doubtful. You're better off taking aspirin in the cheaper form. The gum is useful to people who have trouble swallowing pills.

Moistening the air with a vaporizer will also relieve pain. In addition, the vaporizer, if you use it regularly, may help prevent you from getting a sore throat again. The theory: Low humidity dries out your nasal membranes. Dry membranes are less effective at protecting your body from germs. Keeping the membranes moist enables them to protect you better.

STOMACH ACHES

"What do you take for an upset stomach?" "Alka-Seltzer" is everyone's answer. Wrong. Very wrong. I called 20 stomach doctors (gastroenterologists, they call themselves) and asked them, "Would you recommend Alka-Seltzer for an upset stomach?" All 20 said no. Their objection: Alka-Seltzer has aspirin in it and aspirin can make your stomach bleed. Imagine this scenario: your stomach aches because you have a bleeding ulcer. You take Alka-Seltzer and the aspirin in it kills the ulcer pain. But the aspirin also increases your stomach bleeding. Three hours later, the pain-killing effect of the aspirin wears off and your stomach hurts more than ever. You take more Alka-Seltzer. Your stomach bleeds more. . . . The point: Never take an aspirin product for stomach pain. Aspirin-containing stomach remedies include Alka-Seltzer and Fizrin.

Alka-Seltzer and Fizrin also contain baking soda. In fact, Alka-Seltzer is nothing more than aspirin and baking soda. Baking soda is a decent antacid, and you get a safe dose of it by buying Brioschi, Eno, Bromo Seltzer or Alka-Seltzer Gold (Alka-Seltzer Gold is Alka-Seltzer without aspirin). All of these products are high in salt, however, so don't take them if you have high blood pressure or if you're on a low-salt diet.

A panel of doctors appointed by the FDA to study antacids concluded that Tums and Rolaids are effective antacids, but both can be dangerous if taken too often. Don't exceed the dose recommended on the container, and don't take Rolaids at all if you are on a low-salt diet.

The FDA's panel said that the best and safest antacids are the ingredients in Gelusil, Digel, Maalox, Mylanta and WinGel.

INSOMNIA

Occasional insomnia is common. Everyone can't sleep sometimes. But some of us can't sleep all of the time. That's chronic insomnia. If sleeplessness lasts more than two weeks, you should consult a doctor. However, many people who think they are insomniacs are really getting all the sleep they need. Some people need only five hours' sleep a night, while others need ten. Unless you are terribly tired during the day, what's wrong with sleeping less? Also, studies have shown that many people who think they lie awake tossing and turning are really sleeping pretty soundly. When their sleeping was watched, it was found that people who said, "I hardly slept at all," actually slept six hours or more.

SLEEPING PILLS

Mostly bad news here. Most of the sleep drugs you can buy without a prescription are *not* classified "safe" or "effective" by the FDA. An FDA panel of experts studied Sominex, Sleep-eze, Nytol, Nervine, etc., and was not convinced that they work. The FDA has given its seal of approval to only one drug: Unisom. It contains an anti-allergy drug that (as a side effect) may make you drowsy.

There are some prescription pills that do work, but after a few weeks of regular use, they lose their effectiveness. People build up a tolerance to them, so the long-term insomniac really isn't being helped. Doctors, nevertheless, will continue writing prescriptions because the patient believes in the pill and wants it. Patients may then find that when they do stop using the drug, they get nervous or have nightmares, and have even more insomnia from withdrawal.

Alcohol is another substance people swallow to fight insomnia. Some doctors even suggest a "nightcap" instead of a prescription. Alcohol can relax you and make you sleepy, but it wears off quickly. Then sleeping can be disturbed and sporadic. People build up a tolerance to alcohol, and must take more each night to fall asleep.

A much safer drink is milk. Warm milk at bedtime has long been touted as a sleep-aid, and now there is some research that indicates why it is effective. There is an amino acid in milk, which when taken alone in tests helped people fall asleep and sleep longer.

Sleep tips: There are a number of things you can do to help yourself sleep better. Develop regular bed habits: follow the same pattern before you go to sleep (i.e., ten pushups, then reading). Go to bed at the same time every night. You can train your body to get into the "habit" of going to sleep at a certain time.

If you cannot sleep, don't lie in bed feeling frustrated. Get up, get out of bed and do something (like reading). When you feel drowsy, try sleeping again. If you can't, don't worry. Missing a night or two of sleep does not have serious effects. Worrying about it can just prolong the period of sleeplessness.

Beware of certain drinks before bedtime. You may be taking anti-sleep drugs, without knowing it. Food companies put caffeine in all sorts of products. Coffee and tea have it, of course, but you may not know it's also in chocolate and most soft drinks (Coke, Pepsi, RC Cola, Diet-Rite, Dr. Pepper, Tab, orange soda). If a food contains caffeine, it will be stated on the ingredient label. Many diet pills also contain caffeine. Anacin and Excedrin contain caffeine too.

ASPIRIN AND ASPIRIN SUBSTITUTES

I better not say much about this, because the last time I did, Bristol-Myers sued me for $25,000,000. Bristol-Myers makes Bufferin and Excedrin. Lawsuits aren't supposed to restrict free speech, but of course they do. My lawyer tells me not to talk about aspirin now because my words might be taken out of context and used against me in court.

So I hold my tongue. But here's part of what I said about aspirin on TV:
(The following is an abridged and edited transcript of John Stossel's reports on aspirin, which aired on WCBS-TV News, *The Six O'Clock Report*.)

WEDNESDAY, OCTOBER 10, 1979

John Stossel: If the FTC has its way, we may soon see some interesting changes in aspirin ads. The new commercials could say something like this: (Stossel on camera, dressed as a doctor, imitating aspirin commercials.)

"Contrary to prior advertising, it has not been established that Bayer is any more effective than any other aspirin. . . .

"In the case of Excedrin, it has not been established that Excedrin is more effective for the relief of minor pain . . ."

And so on. The FTC is also asking that corrective ads be run for Anacin, Bufferin, Cope, Vanquish, Midol, and Arthritis Pain Formula. All these drugs are made by just three companies— Bristol-Myers, American Home Products and Sterling Drugs. The FTC says these companies have misled us by spending millions of dollars making scientific sounding claims for their products. Bristol-Myers says it has studies that support its claims. American Home and Sterling Drugs say they won't comment while the matter is in court.

I'd always thought there was something funny about those claims. I mean, how could they *all* be the best and work the fastest. An FDA (Food and Drug Administration) panel of medical experts concluded that there's no proof any brand works better than plain, cheap aspirin, and that products like these [Stossel shows Excedrin, Vanquish, Cope] which contain a combination of ingredients may be even worse for you because they kill no more pain but increase the chance of side effects.

Pain studies are sort of wishy-washy, because there's no precise way to test pain. All they do is hand someone a pill and say: "Hey, would you rate your pain from one to five?" Or: "How do you feel now?"

Norman Kahn (Professor of Pharmacology, Columbia University Medical School): "We can only rely on the patients describing what their feelings are."

Stossel: "As a result you have studies showing one brand works best and other studies contradicting?"

Norman Kahn: "It's—it's very easy to influence the patients."

Stossel: "Today, the commercials make fewer specific claims. Anacin no longer claims to relieve tension. How could it anyway? Anacin contains caffeine, and caffeine can increase tension. The FTC is concerned that years of false claims have *so* misled people, that *stopping* the claims isn't enough; there must be *corrective* advertising. Corrective ads aren't new. Listerine was forced to say Listerine will not prevent colds. S.T.P. had to run ads telling the public it had to pay the government $700,000 because of inaccurate past advertisements.

Actor in Arthritis Pain Formula Commercial: "Do you have anything for headaches?"

Second Actor: "Yeah. Take two of these."

Stossel: But so far, the aspirin companies are not giving in. It's easy to see why. Anacin alone would have to spend $24,000,000 on corrective ads. So through legal moves, they have so far successfully delayed having to run the ads for six years. The government filed the suit in 1973.

And we pay for it all, of course. Our taxes pay the FTC lawyers. We pay the aspirin company lawyers whenever we buy aspirin.

Friday, October 12, 1979

Jim Jensen (Anchorman): A Federal Trade Commission judge ruled today that it has not been established that Bufferin will relieve your pain any faster or that Excedrin is any stronger than aspirin. And, the judge wants Bristol-Myers, the manufacturer, to renounce advertising claims saying its products are faster or stronger. The company says it will appeal [it since has appealed] the ruling which it calls erroneous. Our Consumer Editor, John Stossel's, been reporting on aspirin and advertising this week, and this evening he's here with part three of his series. John . . .

John Stossel: As drugs go, aspirin is pretty terrific. For years it's killed pain or reduced fever and seldom caused unwanted side effects. But some problems do come up. For example, aspirin can cause your stomach to bleed. Gerald Torsiello broke his hip, had surgery, then took aspirin to relieve the pain. He says it relieved the pain, but it also made his stomach bleed.

Gerald Torsiello, Parsippany, New Jersey: "I passed out—right. I passed out. . . ."

John Stossel: "From loss of blood. . . ."

Gerald Torsiello: "From loss of blood. I'd lost three pints of blood."

John Stossel: "Just from taking aspirin."

Gerald Torsiello: "Just from taking aspirin—right."

John Stossel: Actually, it was Anacin, but any aspirin can cause stomach bleeding. Torsiello sued Anacin, saying the label doesn't give warning.

Andy Napolitano, Torsiello's Attorney: "Anacin's attitude, John, basically was that the labeling was sufficient. The label says, "if pain persists for more than ten days or if redness is present. . . ," whatever that means, ". . . consult a physician." It doesn't say, "don't take eight tablets a day for 14 months. It might burn a hole in your stomach, . . ." which is what happened here.

Stossel: At first, Anacin fought him in court, but then decided to settle. I don't know how much they paid him, because the condition of the payment was that he wouldn't talk about it.

Andy Napolitano: "I suspect that they don't want people to know for fear that it will induce a large number of lawsuits."

Stossel: There are *ways* to take aspirin that reduce the problem.

[Bufferin, Cope, Arthritis Pain Formula] contain buffers that, say the companies, make it less likely the aspirin will cause stomach bleeding. Maybe, say the experts.

More effective are products [Bromo Seltzer, Alka-Seltzer, Brioschi] that dissolve before they get to your stomach. However, these are all high in salt, and so not for you if you're on a low salt diet.

If you take the aspirin in pill form, to protect your stomach, you should take it with a full glass of water. Or eat something. That works too.

The best selling pain killer is no longer Bayer. It's now

Tylenol. Aspirin substitutes—Tylenol is just the best known [Camera shows Tylenol, Datril, and Anacin 3]—have become big sellers for some good reasons. They don't cause stomach bleeding. And some people are allergic to aspirin. And. . . .

Actress in Tylenol Commercial: "Do you ever have any difficulty swallowing pills?"

Second Actress: "When I have to swallow a pill, it would stick in my throat."

First Actress: "What would you say about a new extra strength pain reliever that's a liquid?"

Second Actress: "Wowwwwww!! . . ."

Stossel: Aspirin substitutes are available in liquid form. Aspirin will not stay stable in liquid. However, medical experts say it's foolish to avoid aspirin. For one, it's cheaper. Two, stomach bleeding is not a problem for most people. Three, the FDA panel says that, although some acetaminophen advertising suggests the substitutes are safer than aspirin, there is no basis for that claim. And, four, if you have arthritis, well, let Bayer say it. . . .

Announcer in Bayer Commercial: "For arthritis pain, doctors recommend aspirin four to one over any other non-prescription medication."

John Stossel: If you have arthritis, inflammation is part of the problem. Aspirin will reduce inflammation. Aspirin substitutes will not.

Now, Jim had mentioned earlier than an F.T.C. judge ruled today that advertising for these products will have to change. This one [HOLDS UP BUFFERIN] has not been proven to be gentler, nor this one [HOLDS UP EXCEDRIN] stronger than plain aspirin. Bristol-Myers, which makes them, does not agree with that.

Tuesday, October 16, 1979

Jim Jensen (Anchorman): The Bristol-Myers Pharmaceutical Company today filed a $25,000,000 libel suit against CBS and Consumer Editor John Stossel. . . . At a Manhattan news conference, Bristol-Myers vice-president Harry Levine said that Stossel's special reports, "The Truth about Aspirin," made reckless and false statements about advertising claims for Bufferin and Excedrin.

Harry Levine, Bristol-Myers vice-president: "We believe that Mr. Stossel's performance is very simply bad reporting. It is false. It is malicious, and it attacks the good name of our company.

Jim Jensen: Neil Derrough, vice-president and General Manager of WCBS-Television had this response: "We believe that our report . . . did not violate the legal rights of Bristol-Myers.

"WCBS-TV is proud of its consumer reporting, which we consider a valuable public service."

SAVING YOUR SKIN

The hype in the skin-care business is incredible. Never have people paid so much for so little. You can pay up to $200 for some skin-care products, yet skin doctors say Crisco works just as well.

WRINKLES

Getting rid of wrinkles ("Keep Young!") is the main advertising pitch. Clinique La Prarie even operates on pregnant sheep to make skin creams out of sheep embryos. The "youth" of the baby sheep is supposed to be absorbed into your skin. "Total hogwash," said every skin doctor I consulted.

They had about the same opinion of other expensive skin-care creams. First, skin creams won't remove wrinkles. Nothing short of plastic surgery does that (plastic surgery hides the wrinkles by tightening the skin). Wrinkled skin is skin in which the elastic has broken, like an old rubber band. No cream repairs the elastic. No cream even gets deep enough to touch the elastic, despite claims of "deep penetration." Creams cannot even prevent future wrinkling. Wrinkling is caused by age, smiling, frowning, and exposure to sunlight.

There are creams that will *temporarily* remove wrinkles.

These creams (Line-Tamer is a better known brand) contain a chemical that causes your skin to swell temporarily. The swelling tightens the skin and hides the wrinkles (like plastic surgery does). The swelling lasts, however, only eight hours.

Companies keep turning out skin potions because they make an enormous profit on them. The manufacturer of Line-Tamer admits its ingredients aren't very expensive, yet it sells for $72 per ounce. Many cosmetic ingredients cost less than the bottle they are packaged in. The biggest part of the price goes to profit and hype. Cosmetic companies often find that the more they charge, the more they sell. People believe expensive is better. It isn't better.

What *do* you need?

"Plain soap and water," said *every* medical doctor we asked. Fancy facial clinics say you shouldn't use soap. I think they tell you that because they're trying to sell you their own expensive creams. Doctors say soap is fine, although you should be sure to rinse it off thoroughly. If you have dry skin, however, soap may make it drier, so put on a moisturizer after you wash. Use it *immediately* after you wash—the moisturizer is better absorbed when your pores are still open from the warm water.

To remove makeup (or if you don't like using soap) there are the cleansing creams. Here we return to the realm of hype. Doctors tell me Crisco (or any vegetable oil) works as well as expensive department-store creams, yet cosmetic companies make millions selling the expensive stuff. Although Crisco does work, it doesn't smell or feel so great. Smell and feel would be a logical reason to pay more for a product, but Consumers Union found you don't need to pay more. Consumers Union had 147 actors and actresses (they use a lot of stage makeup) test 33 cleansing creams. Consumers Union said no cleanser, whether lotion or cream, rinse-off or wipe-off, proved superior in performance. As for feel, smell, and convenience, most expensive department-store versions got lower ratings than the dime-store products. The top rated:

PRODUCT	COST/OZ.
1. Pond's Light Greaseless Whipped Cold Cream	53¢
2. Revlon Clean & Clear Face Bath (Normal to Oily Skin)	33¢
3. Helena Rubinstein Ultra Feminine Cleansing Cream	76¢
4. Elizabeth Arden Skin Deep Milky Cleanser	63¢
5. Ultima II Milky Facial Bath	81¢
6. Happy Face Facial Washing Cream	28¢

Department-store products that cost as much as $1 to $2 per ounce (one costs $2.75) were rated much lower. I suggest you try the cheapest products until you find one you like.

SKIN TREATMENTS

I like reporting on facial salons. Last time we filmed, I had the chicken embryo facial. You pay $50 for the privilege of having fertilized egg yolks rubbed onto your face. It feels wonderful. It's also totally stupid, according to every skin doctor I consulted.

Facial salons survive on hocus-pocus. People know so little about skin care, there's so much puffery published by the "ladies magazines," there's so much fear about looking old, that some people pay almost anything for ridiculous skin treatments, if the treatments are presented cleverly. Medical accuracy is irrelevant. As long as the salon is luxurious and expensive, people will believe. It helps if you throw in scientific-sounding bunk, like "fertilized chicken eggs." The creative director of Elizabeth Arden admits it:

Pablo Manzoni: "Of course we sell illusions. I feel any woman with a little bit of a complex will go for anything that promises glamour and beauty and a fascinating life-style. She should be entitled to her illusions. Why not?"

No reason why not, if you have money to burn. The treatment is delightful, and you get a clean face out of it. But that's all you get. Doctors say the "deep pore cleansing," the mud packs, the electric gadgets, etc., are all no more effective than a thorough cleansing using soap and water. In addition, some salons give out advice that, according to skin doctors, is incorrect. At one famous salon, the owner told me that people with dry skin should not use much moisturizer because moisturizers "make the oil glands lazy," and cause the glands to produce even less moisture. Doctors say this is nonsense, "The glands are affected by hormones and stress, not moisturizers."

In summary, if you've got lots of money and like to be pampered in luxurious surroundings, go to a salon. But don't expect them to have any magical treatment that will make your skin look younger. And don't depend on the advice they give you. If you have a skin problem, go to a dermatologist.

ACNE

Acne occurs because clogged pores prevent the skin's oils from escaping. It happens most often during adolescence because the skin produces more oil then.

Cancer researchers recently stumbled across a drug that seems to cure acne. Unfortunately, the drug is still undergoing tests, and is not yet available to the public. Antibiotic and hormone treatments, Vitamin A acid, cortisone injections, and cold quartz light therapy have all had some success against acne, but these treatments are only for severe cases. If you have severe acne, see a dermatologist.

For the rest of us, there are drugstore acne preparations. They do work, although not that well. Most of them dry up some of the oils and help unclog the pores by peeling off the top layer of skin.

Keeping your face clean will help too, although washing more than three times a day may be more irritating than helpful. The *type* of soap probably doesn't matter. *The Medicine Show,* Consumer Union's excellent medical advice book, says: "Heavily advertised cleaning products such as Noxzema skin cream, pHisoDerm Medicated Liquid, and Cuticura Medicated Soap are no more useful than a bar of plain soap." Plain soap is much cheaper.

Now that I've written all those nasty things about facial salons, let me contradict myself to say, if you have acne, a facial might help. During the facial they pop pimples "scientifically" (the way a doctor does it). "Scientifically" means the popping is done under sterile conditions, so the pimple doesn't get infected. The facial cleans out your pores, and might prevent some pimples from developing. But it's no cure for severe acne.

Some good news: There's no proof that eating fried foods, candy, peanuts, or chocolate makes acne worse. Making acne sufferers miserable by denying them their favorite foods is unnecessary. You may have an acne-causing reaction to certain foods, but chocolate is no more likely to cause the reaction than spinach. Cosmetics are far more likely to cause acne than food. Avoid heavy makeup. It clogs your pores.

SUN TANNING

A good "healthy" tan! Where did that expression come from? Probably from the days when the malnourished poor worked indoors, in factories, while the rich fiddled around outside playing polo.

We now know that getting a tan is not so healthful. Skin has elastic in it. Sun *ages* skin by destroying that elasticity—it's the same process that shrivels a rubber band if you leave it out in the hot sun. Sun-exposed skin becomes "loose" two to three times faster than unexposed skin. "I used to work in Miami," says one doctor. "I'd see people whose skin looked like elephant skin, but their rear ends, which hadn't seen the sun, looked like the skin of a baby. Even people in their twenties can develop leathery skin by spending a lot of time in the sun."

Prolonged exposure to sun also causes skin cancer. Truck and taxi drivers frequently get skin cancer on their left arms (that's the arm they lean out the window). If you already have a tan, or if you are dark skinned, you're less susceptible. In fact, Blacks almost never get skin cancer. Light/dark skin differences don't apply to everyone, however, Some dark-skinned people burn easily and some light-skinned people are burn-resistant. Regardless of your skin color, if you burn easily, you are more susceptible to skin cancer.

Skin cancer is one of the least dangerous forms of cancer. It rarely kills. Usually, a surgeon simply cuts the cancer out, and you can go back to your regular schedule with hardly a scar to show for your trouble. It's better if the cancer is caught early, so whenever you have a sore that doesn't heal, a discoloration on your skin, or a mole that changes shape or color, see a skin doctor quickly.

Using a reflector increases the sun's damage. Recently a New Jersey woman covered a lounge chair with aluminum foil, fell asleep on the chair and, three hours later, died of sunstroke. Snow, sand and water act as natural reflectors. Snow is a strong reflector; water and sand are weak reflectors. Certain chemicals may also increase sun damage. If you take tranquilizers or birth control pills, or wear perfume or after-shave lotion, you increase the chance the sun will do something bad to your skin.

LOTIONS

Most suntan lotions will protect you from the sun's damage by blocking some or most of the ultraviolet rays before they can touch your skin. The best known protectors are the PABA creams, but plenty of lesser known ingredients offer protection as well. Generally you can tell by the name (Eclipse, Solbar, and Block Out). Some companies now put numbers on their products, like "Coppertone 4." The higher the number, the more protection. "Coppertone 4" means only a fourth of the sun's rays will penetrate.

Contrary to what the advertisements *seem* to say, none of the protecting lotions will give you a "faster" or "darker" tan. If you read the ads closely, you'll notice they no longer make those claims. The protecting lotions protect by screening out some harmful ultraviolet rays. Unfortunately, the harmful rays are also the rays that tan you. By screening out burning rays, you also screen out tanning rays. Sorry; less damage, less tan.

Some lotions offer *no* sunburn protection. These include

Hawaiian Tropic's Dark Tanning Oil, Professional Tanning Oil, Royal Tanning Blend, and Bain de Soleil's Tropical Deluxe Dark Tanning Oil. If you grease yourself with these products you may tan (or burn, or get skin cancer) a little faster than if you use no lotion at all. The oil forms "a lens effect" that actually magnifies the effect of the ultraviolet light. You can accomplish the same thing for less money by smearing on baby oil (adding iodine to the baby oil does nothing), olive oil, or coconut oil. The oil also moistens your skin so there's less sun-drying and therefore less chance of peeling. The moisturizing, however, *has nothing to do* with preventing wrinkles. The wrinkles caused by the sun occur deep in the skin. Adding oil and moisturizers doesn't affect them.

A safer way to get a faster tan is to use one of those indoor–outdoor lotions, like QT. However, those products give you only a fake tan. They dye your skin somewhat like the way the white of an apple turns brown when you expose it to air. The dye doesn't always create a natural-looking tan—sometimes in fact, it makes you look like an apple that's been exposed to air. It may also dye your clothing.

The hour in which you go out in the sun affects the amount of exposure you'll get. You'd think the hottest part of the day, midafternoon, would be when the sun is strongest. In truth, the sun is most powerful when it's highest in the sky: between 12 and 1 o'clock. Likewise, the hot days of August are not powerful sun days. You get the rays most directly around June 21st, the longest day of the year. Therefore, you get as much exposure on cool April 21 as hot August 21.

The sun is also stronger at high altitudes, because there's less atmosphere filtering out the ultraviolet rays. Where there's air pollution you get less sun because the pollution blocks some rays.

Sunlamps work to some extent. They do reproduce the ultraviolet tanning rays. But be careful. Lots of people burn themselves overusing sunlamps. If you replace a sunlamp bulb, remember that the new bulb gives off lots more radiation than the old. Start slowly.

Exposure to sun isn't all bad. Dermatologists say mild exposure may help relieve acne and psoriasis. Sun helps your skin produce Vitamin D (although 5 minutes a day is plenty). Also, lying out in the sun feels good, so what the hell.

HAIR CARE: SHAMPOOS; LOSING HAIR; SHAVING

Remember the old saying: "Brush your hair 100 times in the morning to keep it looking good?" Wrong. It doesn't stimulate hair growth, improve scalp circulation, or do anything useful for your hair. Brush your hair 100 times in the morning and you'll end up breaking it and pulling it out.

When hair is wet, never comb or brush it roughly. Wet hair is very breakable. Brush it gently or wait for it to dry.

If you use a blow-dryer, keep it moving. If you hold it in one spot, or put it extra close to your hair to make it dry faster, the heat will damage the hair.

Shampoos. What a hype! Wella Corporation pays Jaclyn Smith $100,000 + to say, "Switch to Wella Balsam . . . You'll love your hair," etc. Yet hair experts say it doesn't really matter what brand of shampoo you pick. All that's important is to pick an "oily hair" shampoo if your hair is oily, a "dry hair" shampoo if your hair is dry. To tell what type of hair you have, rub a tissue against your hair three hours after you shampoo. If there's oil on the tissue, you have oily hair. If not, you have dry hair. Dry hair also tends to have a lot of static electricity, and be more "fly away." Most shampoos are labeled "oily" or "dry." Not all oily or dry shampoos will work equally well on *your* hair. You may have to try different ones until you find the best for you.

PH or no pH? Shampoo ads brag about this or that product having "just the right pH" for your hair. Experts we consulted say these claims are meaningless. All shampoos have about the same pH.

Vitamins? Ads about "vitamin shampoos" are also meaningless. Adding vitamins won't make your hair healthier, nor stop it from falling out. If you're losing your hair because of a vitamin deficiency, your teeth would be falling out too. "Head Start" vitamins have been in trouble with the government for years. The Postal Service has now forced them to stop claiming Head Start will stop baldness.

Dandruff: Dandruff shampoos do work, but you should change brands every several months. In time your scalp becomes resistant to one brand, and the dandruff will return.

Protein: Protein added to shampoo won't work any miracles, but it can do some good. The protein can coat damaged hair and make it look nicer.

Conditioners: Conditioners do work. If you bleach, dye, straighten, or permanent your hair the outer layer is probably damaged. A conditioner smoothes out some of the damage.

The experts we consulted said it doesn't really matter which brand you pick. There's no such thing as "deep conditioning." The conditioning only lasts until the next rinse. Leaving the conditioner on extra long doesn't help either. The ones you keep on for half and hour and the ones you wash off in two minutes have roughly the same formulas.

Hair dyes. Do the dyes cause cancer? Maybe. Rats that ate some of the dyes got cancer. Of course we don't eat hair dye. However, it was found that when the dyes were painted on to the rats' backs, they absorbed the dye. It came out in their urine.

The suspect chemicals are most likely to be found in dark dyes, less likely in shades of red or blond. Most companies have now removed the suspect chemicals. If one of those chemicals is in a dye, it will say so somewhere on the label.

1. 4-Methoxy-M-Phenylene Diamone
2. 2-Nitro-Phenylene Diamone
3. 4-Chloro-M-Phenylene Diamone
4. 4-Amino-2-Nitro Phenol
5. 2, 4 Diamino Toluene

Losing your hair: Hair falls out all the time. That's no problem for most people, because new hairs grow right back. If your hair is falling out and not regrowing, blame your ancestors. They gave you genes that are now telling your hair follicles: "Forget it; we don't need any more hair." If this is the cause of your baldness, there is nothing you can do about it.

It's possible that your baldness is caused by some curable disease. Possible, but not likely. Baldness in women may be a hormone problem. If you want to check this out, do *not* go to a "hair clinic" or a trichologist. They'll most likely sell you some lotion or plausible-sounding treatment ("We'll massage your scalp with these electrodes and that will restore lost circulation. . . .") that is, in fact, worthless. To see if your baldness is curable, go to a dermatologist.

In 99% of the cases, the baldness is inherited. All you can do is buy a wig, a hair weave, implants, or transplants.

Wigs: Actually, "hairpiece" is a better description, since it just covers the bald parts. A wig is a total substitute set of hair. The best-looking hairpieces tend to be custom-made. They cost about $400.

The hairpiece designer covers your scalp with masking tape. When he pulls it off, the tape forms a cap that matches the shape of your bald part. From that they make the "piece." Sometimes they use real hair, from Italian or Far Eastern women who earn extra money growing their hair long and selling it. They don't use Americans' hair because it's usually not in as good shape: too many Americans dye and tease their hair. Many shops use synthetic hair. They say it holds color better and tangles less than real hair.

It you don't want to pay for a custom piece, you can buy good off-the-rack models for about $150 (the range is $50 to $350). The stylist will show you several models and try to comb your real hair around it. Some off-the-rack hairpieces look as good as custom jobs.

Hairpieces aren't the jokes they used to be. Good ones make it look like you have your own hair. You can wear them in the shower and go swimming with them. If you are still insecure about the wig falling off, maybe you'd like a hair weave. Maybe.

Hair weaves: A weave is simply a hairpiece that is woven to what real hair you have. First they braid your hair tightly. Then they sew the hairpiece to the braid. It isn't cheap: about $1,000 for the initial weave and piece. Many people like weaves because they are more secure than ordinary hairpieces. Some hockey players wear them so they won't be embarrassed if somebody pulls their hair during a fight.

However, I think weaves are more aggravation than benefit. Because your own hair grows out, the weave starts coming loose every six weeks or so. Then you have to return to the weaver for a $40 retightening. Weaves are also hard to clean. Some weave wearers say they have to use a shower massage device to wash their scalps.

Implants: Don't do it. Implants are artificial hairs sewn into the scalp. It sounds reasonable. The ads say: "NO AWKWARD HAIRPIECES, PERMANENT HAIR PAINLESSLY!" They lie.

Dr. Marvin Lepaw, Dermatologist: "I'm sorry. I know it's painful. . . ."

Stossel (to audience): This doctor is removing hair implanted by the Syntho Hair Clinic. . . .

Unidentified Doctor: ". . . hang in. Yeah—that came out nicely. . . ."

Stossel (to audience): These patients—wearing masks because they're ashamed to reveal their identities—say Syntho promised painless hair replacement, but gave them incredible pain and infections.

Unidentified Patient #1 in Mask: "And I says to them, please help me. Take the hair out. I just can't take it no more. We went into the examining room. They looked at me. They says you're right. Some of this hair has to come out. He pulled and yanked. And the pain was unbearable."

Stossel (to audience): "The implant cost $3,000. . . ."

Second Unidentified Patient in Mask: "I'm out $3,000. I have an infected head. They refuse to give the money back . . ."

Dr. Marvin Lepaw: "It would seem incomprehensible that anyone who calls himself a doctor would ever leave sutures or synthetic material in the skin, and not be aware of the fact that these sutures will ultimately lead to infection and rejection by the body . . ."

Unidentified Patient #2 in Mask: "They just ruined me. They—they just—I guess I'll have to wear something over my head for the rest of my life."

Stossel (to audience): The owner of Syntho is Ivan Ruben. He didn't return our calls, so I dropped by his office. . . .

Ivan Ruben, Owner, Syntho Hair Clinic: "There's no comment I can make at the present moment."

Stossel: "Well, what about these people, and look what's happened to their—to their heads. It's pretty horrible. And you're still advertising for more people to come in and have this done to them?"

Ivan Ruben: "Well, I have no comment at this present moment. . . ."

Stossel (to audience): The State Health Department is now investigating implant clinics. They suspect that some of the surgery is being done by unlicensed people under non-sterile conditions.

A few days after that confrontation, Ruben closed the Syntho Clinic and disappeared. Other implant clinics have opened and closed. Sometimes health bureaucrats go after them, but usually only after dozens of people have been injured.

Doctors say it is stupid to sew artificial hairs onto anyone's head. The body mobilizes its defenses (the same defenses that fight disease) and rejects the hairs. As a result—infection, pain, and the artificial hairs must be removed, one by one. New clinics still open from time to time. Don't fall for it. A safer way to cover a bald spot surgically is *trans*plants.

Transplants: Don't confuse them with implants, above. Transplants are just what they sound like. A doctor (usually a dermatologist) takes some hair from where you have it (usually the back of your head) and replants it in your bald spot. It's like repotting a plant. The operation is usually done in a doctor's office, not a hospital. It's painful.

Stossel (to audience): The patient is awake. Only his scalp is anesthetized. The doctor takes a drill with a hollow bit. . . .
Dr. Herb Feinberg: "You'll hear this buzzing sound, and you will feel nothing—just a bit of pressure . . ."
Stossel (to audience): He digs about 20 holes in the back of the patient's head. . . ."
Dr. Herb Feinberg: "I'm going to be taking out the individual grafts . . ."
Stossel (to audience): Each graft is a piece of scalp about the size of a pea. It has about 10 hairs in it. The graft will grow hair wherever you put it, even on the soles of your feet if you want it to, because it's programmed to grow scalp hair.
Stossel (to audience): He digs 20 holes in the top of the patient's head . . . and places the grafts inside them.
Stossel (to patient): "Why do you want to have this done?"
Patient: "I like myself better with hair. And—just vanity, I guess . . ."

A transplant costs from $1,000 to $2,500, depending on the size of the bald spot. It's not fun. They don't do all the transplants at one time, so you have to keep coming back. Maybe five times. The hair may take months to grow in. Sometimes only a few hairs grow in each plug; then it looks like you have polka-dots on your head. On the other hand, many transplant patients are delighted with their new hair, and glad they had the operation.

Shaving: While I'm talking about hair, some comments on getting rid of it.

Q: Why do you use shaving cream?
A: To soften the whiskers, so they'll be easier to cut.

That's what everybody thinks, but that's not really the way it works. It's the water that softens the hairs. All shaving cream does is hold the water to your face. It takes a minute and a half for the water to work (to cause maximum softness), so keep your face wet that long. If you shave in the shower, you don't need shaving cream.

Does shaving cause hairs to grow back faster and coarser? No, according to the Japanese, who ran a fancy research study where they took 100 men and shaved the hairs on one side of their chests. With microscopes, they watched the shaven and unshaven chest hairs grow. The result: No difference in growth.

Women who remove hair by waxing instead of shaving their legs may notice that the hair grows back more slowly. That's because waxing takes the hair out below skin level.

TEETH AND TOOTHPASTE

KEEPING YOUR TEETH

Do you worry about tooth decay? If you want to worry about something, I'd worry more about gum decay. Because of gum decay, 20,000,000 Americans (1 in 11 people) have *no teeth* at all. There's a good chance that you'll lose your teeth by the time you turn 65.

It doesn't have to be that way. The brushing and flossing you do to prevent cavities will also protect your gums, *if* you brush and floss correctly. The *way* you brush is far more important

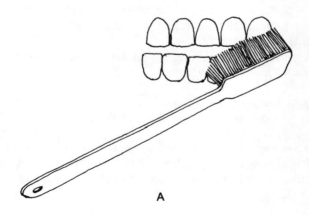

A

than which toothpaste you use. The correct way is probably *not* the way you are doing it if you were taught before the mid 1970s. Today dentists teach people to hold the brush at a 45° angle (see picture A) and jiggle the brush around the gum line. The idea is to gently dislodge the garbage that's collecting around the gums. You don't want to scrub back and forth (you're not polishing a floor) because that misses the harmful stuff's hiding places. The jiggle technique works best with a soft bristle brush. A hard brush might damage your gums.

A toothbrush doesn't reach between the teeth, so you need dental floss. Don't just jam the floss between the teeth. Work on each side of the tooth separately (see picture B). pull the floss back and forth. Unwaxed floss cleans best because it provides more friction, but waxed floss is more pleasant (and less likely to snag).

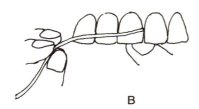

B

The goal is to get rid of plaque. Plaque is the stuff that forms when food particles mix with saliva. Plaque will eventually eat into your tooth (causing cavities) and gums (causing them to withdraw from your teeth). If you brush your teeth correctly, one brushing a day is enough to get rid of plaque. If you do it wrong, three brushings won't be enough.

Toothpaste: The American Dental Association gives its seal of approval to Aim, Aqua-Fresh, Colgate MFP, Crest, and Macleans. That means those companies showed the ADA test results indicating those toothpastes fight cavities, and the ADA believed the tests. Other brands that contain fluoride (it usually says "fluoride" on the label) may work as well. They don't have ADA approval simply because their manufacturers have not gone to the expense and trouble to submit their product to the ADA for evaluation.

In addition to fluoride, toothpastes have little bits of grit known as "abrasives" in them. It's the abrasives that do the cleaning. If there's too little abrasiveness, the toothpaste won't scrape the dirt away . . . too much abrasiveness and you may damage your teeth and gums. The following chart shows which toothpastes are most and least abrasive (the higher the number, the more abrasiveness):

PRODUCT	AVERAGE ABRASIVENESS
Listerine	44
Craig Martin	45
Peak	78
Pepsodent	81
Crest	109
Colgate ASF	109
Ultra-Brite	111
Sensodyne	118
Aim	124
Close-Up	126
Macleans MFP	130
Philips	138
Colgate MFP	141

Source: American Dental Association

If your toothpaste hurts your teeth, try a less abrasive brand (and see your dentist—pain is a sign of trouble). If you have stains on your teeth, try a more abrasive brand. You might also want a less abrasive brand if you brush often and vigorously, a more abrasive brand if you brush lightly. In either case, you probably save a little money by using *less* toothpaste. You don't need to cover the length of the brush. A little toothpaste cleans as well as a lot.

The toothpastes Sensodyne and Themodent are advertised as good "for sensitive teeth." As the chart shows, Sensodyne is not particularly low in abrasiveness, yet both products do contain chemicals that might deaden pain. The American Dental Association says it is not convinced that either really is better for sensitive teeth.

Claims about "whiteners" in toothpaste to give you "sex appeal" are mostly advertising hype. Ultra-Brite, Macleans, Pearl Drops, and Close-Up contain no chemical that will bleach your teeth white.

You know sugar causes tooth decay. If you have a sweet tooth and plan to eat sugar anyway, eat it *with* meals rather than between meals. That reduces the chance of decay because chewing the other foods helps wash the sugar off your teeth.

VITAMINS

"You're wasting your money," says WCBS-TV's Science Editor as he catches me popping a multiple vitamin at the drinking fountain. "Unnecessary," says every medical doctor I consult. "If you eat well, you get all the vitamins you need from food." Okay, maybe that's true. But who eats well? I do sometimes, but certainly not all the time. So I take a multiple vitamin. Why not? It only costs 2¢, and it can't hurt me (although it would be harmful if I took huge amounts of vitamins A or D). When I take more vitamins than I need, they just pass through my body. A waste of money, but no harm.

Health food stores often try to convince people that "natural" vitamins are better. There's no good evidence for that. Synthetic Vitamin C is just as good for you as "natural C" or "rose hips," and much cheaper. All synthetic vitamins are cheaper.

When you take a vitamin pill, take it *during* or *after* a meal, not *before*. Some vitamins need to mix with fat or other vitamins to work properly. Without mixing with their counterpart, they just pass through your body ineffectually. By taking the pill with or after a meal, you mix the vitamin with different foods, and increase the chance it will be properly absorbed.

BODY ODORS

Listening to TV commercials, I wonder how, before deodorants, people could stand each other. How could they eat together, sit next to each other, make love, without "twenty-four-hour protection?" We spend $200,000,000 trying to hide our natural smells. Oh well; if we're going to do it, let's understand how it works.

Sweating itself doesn't make you smell. The smell occurs when minerals in your sweat mix with bacteria prowling around on your skin. Some types of sweat create more smell than others. "Nervous" sweat, for example, has more smell-making chemicals in it than "exercise" sweat. Other things being equal, therefore, you smell worse after a rough job interview than a good workout.

To reduce smell, you must either eliminate the sweat and/or the bacteria, or let the sweat and the bacteria do their thing and drown the result with perfume. Drowning the results is exactly what deodorants do. They apply good smells to the bad. Deodorants also contain some bacteria-killing chemicals. Anti-perspirants go one step further. They contain bacteria-killing chemicals, perfume, *and* a chemical that plugs your pores to keep you from sweating. You can buy a deodorant or anti-perspirant in an aerosol can, stick, roll-on, or whatever, but FDA tests found them *least* effective in aerosol cans. Aerosol spray anti-perspirants work half as well and cost three times as much. Sticks, creams, and roll-ons are better buys. There is also a question about what breathing the spray does to your lungs. If you use the spray type, hold your breath, spray it, and then run out of the room.

FOOT ODOR

If your feet smell, it could be your socks. Synthetic materials hold the sweat in. Try switching from nylon or silk to cotton or wool socks. If your feet still smell, it might be the shoes. Switch from synthetic material to leather. Throw some talc on your feet to absorb the sweat.

MOUTHWASHES

If you have bad breath, mouthwash won't cure it. If you read the ads closely, you'll notice companies no longer claim that. Instead they say only "freshens your breath." It's like putting perfume in your mouth. It drowns out bad smells, but only briefly. Breath mints do about the same thing.

Bad breath doesn't always come from the mouth. If you reek of garlic it's not because you have garlic in your mouth, it's because your lungs take the smell from your blood and blow it out as you breathe. In fact, if you rub garlic on your feet, it will soon smell on your breath.

Some bad breath does start in the mouth. It may be caused by decaying food lodged between the teeth. In that case, flossing does more good than mouthwash. It may be caused by bacteria on the tongue. In that case, brushing or scraping (use a spoon or toothbrush) your tongue will help more than mouthwash. Bad breath may be due to a stomach disorder. Then you need to see a doctor.

VAGINAL SPRAYS AND DOUCHES

Every doctor we consulted said: Don't use them. If your vagina smells bad, it may be an indication of an infection or some other problem. You should go to a gynecologist to ask about it, rather than just masking the smell with a perfume.

To keep clean, soap and water is all you should use. That's for *external* cleaning. Your natural secretions take care of internal cleaning.

Vaginal sprays and douches may be harmful. The sprays sometimes cause skin irritation. The douches dry up your normal secretions and sometimes lead to itching and infection. One of my researchers asked the head of the FDA's panel on gynecological devices, "Why do women use these devices if they do no good and can in fact be harmful?" Said the doctor: "Madison Avenue did a good snow job."

HEARING AIDS

One thousand hearing aids are sold every day. What's sad is that many of the people who buy them cannot be helped by them. At the same time thousands of people who could be helped don't wear them.

A hearing aid is little more than an amplifier, similar to the one you have in your radio, but smaller. Today's amplifiers fit right in your ear: you don't need obnoxious wires leading to the works in your pocket. Many people who would otherwise lead restricted lives are now active and working because they have the proper hearing aid.

The problem: Hearing aids don't just magnify sound, they magnify specific types of sound, so different types of hearing loss require different hearing aids. Also, some types of loss cannot be helped by an aid at all, so don't buy one casually.

For example: If you have trouble hearing because you have a hole in your eardrum, you don't need a hearing aid—you need surgery, which would probably cure you.

Often people try hearing aids and then give up on them: For example:

61-year-old-man: "The dealer said it would help me and it seemed to at first, but then it didn't and I got tired of wearing it."

Stossel: Now the $400 hearing aid sits in a drawer. He lost his job, and collects welfare. He doesn't go out much, because it's tiring trying to figure out what people are saying. Most days he sits at home, alone.

This man was the victim of an incompetent hearing-aid dealer. He could be helped by a hearing aid, but only by a different type from the one he was sold. He'd given up on hearing aids, because he had a bad experience. I arranged to have him tested by an audiologist, who got him a different type of hearing aid. Suddenly he could hear.

Man: "I can't believe it. It's like I've been dead and now I'm alive again. I got my job back. I'm doing things. It's wonderful."

He was fortunate to have been tested by an audiologist. Many people just go to hearing-aid stores. That's crazy. A hearing-aid dealer is a businessman. His goal is not to test your hearing. He's a salesman whose income depends on selling hearing aids. He may have no special training. He may be a former car salesman, for all you know. In most states, almost anybody can open up a hearing-aid store, and some pretty sleazy people do. The N.Y.C. Department of Consumer Affairs once sent investigators with perfect hearing to several hearing-aid dealers. Many of the dealers told the investigators they had faulty hearing and should buy hearing aids. Other tests found dealers trying to sell *two* hearing aids to people with perfect hearing. A hearing aid sells for $400. They cost the dealer only about $130. If you think you are hard of hearing, I suggest that you go to an audiologist. You can find them under "Audiologists" or "Speech and Hearing" in the Yellow Pages, but it would be safer to call a University's "speech pathology" department and ask for a recommendation. An audiologist will charge you about $50, play various beeps in your ear, and tell you whether you need a hearing aid. The audiologist's test is far more thorough than one you'd get in a hearing-aid store. More important, audiologists have no incentive to cheat. Since they don't sell hearing aids, they have no reason to lie to you about your need for one. If you *do* need a hearing aid, the audiologist will give you a prescription you can take to the hearing-aid store.

It might be safest to go to an audiologist who is certified by the American Speech and Hearing Association. But disregard certification by the National Hearing Aid Society. That is merely a trade association of hearing-aid dealers.

To be really safe, you should go to an ear doctor too. They don't usually give hearing tests, but because of their medical training, they can determine whether your hearing loss is caused by a tumor, high blood pressure, diabetes or some other medical problem that needs treatment. The doctor may even find out you can't hear because you've been taking too much aspirin. Take less, and you don't need the hearing aid.

Ear doctors call themselves otolaryngologists. They charge about $35 for an examination.

Before you go to the dealer to buy the hearing aid, call several. Ask if they give 30-day trial periods (all good dealers do). Ask for a discount if you already have your prescription since the dealer doesn't need to give you a hearing test. Go to a dealer who offers the trial period and the discount.

Medicaid pays for hearing aids; Medicare does not.

HAVING AN OPERATION

When I go to the doctor, I think of a friendly expert who has only my interests at heart. Stupid. A physician might have my interests at heart, but is also a businessperson. Builders like to build, ballet dancers like to dance, and surgeons like to cut. Money is one reason. Surgeons don't make much salary; like insurance salesmen, they're paid commissions—the more they cut, the more they earn. Aside from the money, most surgeons like operating.

Unfortunately, what the surgeon likes may not be the best thing for you. Thousands of hemorrhoidectomies are done every year, yet an office procedure that gets rid of the hemorrhoid by squeezing it with a rubber band usually works just as well. Surgeons often remove the breast and lymph nodes of women with breast cancer, although studies show women who receive less radical treatment do just as well.

Next time your surgeon says, "Let's operate," get a second opinion. And don't get it from another surgeon; surgeons are cut-happy. Go to an internist or general practitioner or, better yet, a specialist in your disease. And don't ask *your* doctor to recommend someone—you may be referred to a crony who always rubber-stamps your physician's diagnoses. If you need help finding a doctor for a second opinion, call 800-638-6833. That's a government toll-free hotline; they'll give you a recommendation. Good doctors won't be offended when you say you're double-checking their opinions. They understand that those are the rules of the game. Getting another opinion prevents so many unnecessary operations that Blue Cross/Blue Shield often pays for the second opinion. Medicare now pays for second opinions, and Medicaid pays in most states.

The second opinion is often different from the first opinion. A recent study showed that 43% of the second opinions contradicted the first.

One dramatic case reported recently by *The Washington Post:* A doctor told a 48-year-old Maryland woman that she had inoperable bone cancer, and she should not expect to live more than a year. She immediately quit her job and became so despondent that she broke off relations with her fiancé. She got her adult children to move back into her home as she awaited the end. She planned her funeral. Then she went to a Cancer Center in New York for more tests and was told: She was perfectly healthy; she never had cancer. She sued her doctor and won $800,000 in damages.

Experts say the operations most often done without a real need for them are hemorrhoidectomies, hysterectomies, appendectomies, and tonsillectomies (removing hemorrhoids, uteri, appendixes and tonsils). No one's done studies on it, but I think abortion should be on the list.

ABORTION

If doctor #1 recommends a tonsillectomy and doctor #2 says it's not necessary, it doesn't mean doctor #1 is a cheat. It's a judgment call. Doctor #1 may have really believed the tonsillectomy was necessary. Not so with abortion.

If you think you're pregnant, the doctor does two simple tests. He/she gives you an internal exam to see if the pregnancy can be felt. Then a lab test is run to see if a pregnancy hormone is present in your urine. If the urine test says you are pregnant when you're not, the internal exam will catch the mistake. So the doctor knows: Either you're pregnant or you're not.

I heard that some doctors are so greedy they peform abortions on women who are not pregnant. One gynecologist put it: "Performing abortions on women who aren't pregnant is an ideal moneymaker for a shady doctor. It happens all the time. The woman doesn't know she isn't pregnant, and since she's not, it's an easy operation." ·

We ran a test. Two WCBS researchers went to six abortion doctors for pregnancy tests. Both women had been certified "not pregnant" by several gynecologists. To be extra certain, I had them bring in samples of *my* urine for the tests. Amazingly, 2 of the 6 doctors we tested said both researchers *were* pregnant, and they tried to perform the abortion. The women had to jump off the table and shout, "No, I've changed my mind! I don't want an abortion!" or the doctors would have gone ahead and done it.

We recorded this with hidden cameras and broadcast it. After the broadcast, one of the doctors closed his abortion clinic and disappeared. The other is still practicing. She is Dr. Linda Kim, and she performs abortions on Park Avenue in New York City.

I don't know how often this kind of thing goes on, but it's scary that although we tested only 6 clinics, it happened to us twice. The State Health Department could catch the crooks by running tests like the ones we ran. But they don't do that sort of thing.

THE RIGHT WAY

An early abortion (in the first 12 weeks of pregnancy) is relatively safe. It can be done in a doctor's office with local anesthesia. The doctor uses a vacuum instrument, which simply pulls the fetus from the uterus; $150 is a typical price.

To find a good clinic, I suggest you call a local Planned Parenthood office for a recommendation.

A good clinic will always:

1. Give you both a urine test and an internal examination.
2. Take some of your blood to determine your blood type. If you are Rh negative, you need a shot within 72 hours of the abortion; otherwise you increase the chance that your future children will have birth defects or that you will miscarry.
3. Give you a phone number you can call day or night should something go wrong after the operation.

AT HOME PREGNANCY TESTS

Several companies now sell test kits you use at home. The test is similar to a doctor's urine test. You mix your urine with a chemical in the kit, and wait two hours. If a brown–red color appears, you are probably pregnant; if it doesn't, you're probably not. The kits cost about $12. That's cheaper than going to the doctor. Unfortunately, the kits are less accurate than doctors' tests. If there's a little detergent in the container used to collect the urine, or if you bump the kit while doing the test, it may tell you you're pregnant when you're not. Or vice versa.

On average, if the kit says you are pregnant, you almost certainly are. The kits are right about that 96% of the time. When the kit says you are *not* pregnant, however, it is right only 80% of the time. As a result the kit companies say: If the test says you are not pregnant, but you've skipped a period and have pregnancy symptoms, take the test again. The longer you've been pregnant, the more accurate the test. Doctors think you should be even more careful, because not knowing you are pregnant can be dangerous. They suggest seeing a doctor rather than taking the second test. If you skip two periods, it's certainly time to see a doctor.

BREAST ENLARGEMENT

Whenever I report on breast-building I'm struck by why women say they want bigger breasts. Men in their lives generally don't push them to do it (men's preferences are not what you'd suspect, anyway. *Playboy* pollster Howard Smith surveyed men and found as many prefer small breasts as big). The woman herself feels inadequate. She feels competition with girlfriends, sisters, or women in the media. Being "small" makes the woman feel "not feminine." I think it makes more sense to accept the way you are than pursue bigger breasts. But if you want to get "bigger" there are two approaches:

1. You can have an operation. A plastic surgeon puts silicone bags inside your breasts. This works, but it's scary, costs about $2,000, and often your breasts become as hard as baseballs.

2. You turn to the back of *Cosmopolitan* magazine and, presto, your problems are solved! Send $10 to $20 to this or that company and you'll get a product that will give you the big breasts you've always wanted. It's mostly bunk, but not entirely bunk. We sent away for bust developers advertised in *Cosmopolitan, Redbook,* and *Mademoiselle. (Glamour, Ladies' Home Journal, McCalls, Ms.,* and *Vogue* refuse to carry the ads.)

One company sent a can of "Right Places" protein powder for $10.95. Protein will not build breasts. "Right Places" has since had its mail stopped by the Post Office. Another product cost us $20.95 and turned out to be a piece of plastic shaped like a breast. You attach the plastic to a faucet and it sprays water on your breasts. "Useless, though it might feel good," said the doctors we consulted. Some ads brought us creams to rub in.

Said the doctors: "Also useless." Some companies took our money and sent us nothing (now that's a profitable business). Mark Eden, probably the most famous of the companies, charged us $8 and sent us a hinged piece of plastic with a spring in the middle.

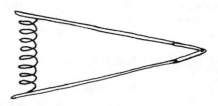

The idea: If you hold the exerciser at arm's length and squeeze it, you enlarge the pectoral muscles in your chest. The exerciser *will* enlarge the pectorals, but that does not enlarge the cup size itself. "Exercise all you want," said one doctor, "it's not going to make your breasts any bigger. Your breast is a gland and fat depository, not a muscle."

Nevertheless, using exercise devices may make your breasts *look* bigger, because building the muscles behind the breasts makes the breasts stick out. You don't need to buy an $8 mail-order device to do that. Squeezing a rubber ball between your hands at arm's length works just as well.

You may be tempted to try hypnosis. Some hypnotists claim that women, under hypnosis, can enlarge their breasts by directing more blood to flow into the breasts.

I interviewed one such hypnotist:

Dr. Thomas Zenat (to woman reclining in chair): "Imagine a warm, hot sun . . ."

Stossel (to audience): Dr. Zenat claims he can make women's breasts grow through hypnotism.

Dr. Zenat (to woman): "Your breasts are feeling warmer . . ."

Stossel (to audience): In a trance, the woman is told to imagine blood flowing to her breasts.

Dr. Zenat: ". . . a warm, pleasant and comfortable . . ."

Stossel (to audience): Dr. Zenat has been traveling the country accompanied by women he's hypnotized. The result?

Woman with Dr. Zenat: "Fantastic. Because now I can go into a store and I can buy a 34B, and believe me, that's a heck of an uplifting for your spirit."

Stossel: "You used to be a . . ."

Woman with Dr. Zenat: "A 32A."

Stossel (to audience): Dr. Zenat now sells self-hypnosis tapes for $45.

Stossel (to Zenat): "Now, a number of doctors, I imagine, would call you a quack. In fact, some hypnotists we called *do* call you a quack. They say you have this traveling road show, that you're trying to sell your kit to get rich."

Dr. Zenat: "I certainly honor and respect their right to an opinion. It's unfortunate that they just don't know what they're talking about."

Stossel (to audience): We talked to five other hypnosis experts. All five said: "No way his treatment will work."

One television footnote: When the interview ended and the camera lights were shut off, Dr. Zenat cussed me out for surprising him with hostile questions (I had also confronted him about his hypnotism credentials. His press release listed him as an officer in several important-sounding organizations. The organizations said he was not an officer), then he stalked out of the room, followed by his entourage of busty women.

Dr. Zenat's reaction was unusual. Usually people I confront hang around to pose for "reverse questions" (news interviews are usually shot with only one camera, which is of course pointed at the subject. After the interview the camera crew moves its gear around to take a picture of me while I ask the same questions I asked before. Those are "reverse questions"). I am constantly amazed how people I confront sit there and pose while I re-ask horribly hostile questions: "Why did you try to abort her when she wasn't pregnant? . . ." "Here are the documents that show you've stolen . . . ." "This tape recording proves you're a liar, doesn't it?" Interview subjects invariably sit politely and deny the charges again as we make these "reverse" shots. Then, even more absurd, they often thank me for the interview, shake hands, and before they leave, ask if there is anything else they can do to help. It's amazing. No one (except Zenat) has gotten mad. No one has said, "To hell with your camera shots! I'm leaving!" It's not that they are afraid to get mad because the camera is on—the camera is *off* while we're switching to the "reverse" position. Perhaps people are so surprised at being directly accused that they go into some kind of "numb" state. The numbness doesn't last long. A few hours later their lawyers are on the phone threatening: "We'll sue if you put that on . . . I'm friends with important people at CBS, you'll be fired, . . . etc." Any psychologists reading this? You should do a research project on it.

BUYING DRUGS

One of the best ways to waste money is to buy brand-name drugs. Suppose you want a tranquilizer. You can buy chlordiazepoxide for $2, or you can buy the *exact same* ingredients under the brand name Librium for $10. $2 vs. $10. And which do people buy most often? You guessed it: the more expensive Librium. Why? Because their doctors write Librium on the prescription pad. Why do doctors do that? In most cases it just doesn't occur to them to worry about an $8 difference on a bottle of pills. The doctor is also more familiar with Librium. Since there are such big markups on brand-name drugs, drug companies advertise them heavily. They have salesmen visit the doctor's office. They bring the doctor gifts. No one makes enough profit on chlordiazepoxide to promote it that way. Also, the doctor has probably prescribed Librium for years and knows how different patients react to it. Why change? The doctor may not even know chlordiazepoxide is a cheaper version of the same drug.

Your pharmacist knows. When you go to the drugstore, ask for the "generic equivalent" of whatever your doctor prescribes. It will contain the same ingredients, but it will cost *much* less. Better yet, bring it up when your doctor writes the prescription. In rare cases, the doctor may not want you to take the generic equivalent. In most cases the response will be "Oh yeah, there is a generic. Let's see, I'll look it up . . . I guess it's cheaper."

Much cheaper. Another example: A bottle of the antibiotic Terramycin costs $30, and crazily outsells tetracycline, which has the *exact same* ingredients and sells for $5.

Whether you buy brand name or generic, it pays to shop around when buying drugs. Terramycin costs $20 at some drugstores I've tried, $45 at others. I know it's a pain to shop around, but it's really worth it. You save pennies price-shopping for food, *dollars* shopping around for drugs.

Finally, your doctor may be prescribing some drugs that simply do not work. Your doctor doesn't know that they're ineffective because physicians don't have time to read all the research. They prescribe them because they've been bamboozled by the drug companies' ads.

The following drugs are still being sold because of various bureaucratic snafus. They are

UNPROVEN DRUGS STILL BEING SOLD DESPITE 1962 LAW BANNING INEFFECTIVE DRUGS

UNPROVEN DRUGS EXEMPT FROM BANNING

Achromycin w/HC, Actified (also -C Expectorant), Adroyd (2.5, 5.,10 mg.), Ambenyl Expectorant, Amodrine, Amphocortrin, Anadrol, Asminyl, Bacitracin-Poly-Ned- HC, Beclysyl with Dextrose, Benadryl with Ephedrine, Beonquin ointment, Bentyl and Bentyl/Phenobarbital, Benylin Expectorant, Berocca-C (also 500), Betolake Forte, Blephamide Liquifilm, Breonex-L and -M.

Caldecort, Cantil w/Phenobarbital, Clor-Trimeton, Cloromycetin-HC, Clistin Expectorant and R-A, Co-Pyronil and co-Pyronil Pediatric, Coditrate, Cor-oticin, Cor-Tar-Quin (0.5 and 1%), Cordran-N, Coricidin/ Codeine, Cortisporin (also -G), Cortomycin, Cremothalidine.

Dactil and Dactil/Phenobarbital, Daricon PB, Deca-Durabolin, Decaspray, Di-Hydrin, Dianabol (2.5 and 5 mg.) Dimetane (also Expectorant and Expectorant DC), Dimetapp (also Extentab), Disomer, Disophrol, Duotrate 45, Durabolin (25 and 50 mg./cc).

Enarax (5 and 10), Erythocin, Florinef-S, Folbesyn, Forhistal, HC .5% (also 1, 1.5, 2.5%) with Neomycin 5 mg., Hispril, Hista-Clopane, Histadyl and Ephed (1 and 2), Histionex 50, Hycodon, Hydrocortisone/ Heomyc, Hydroderm.

Ilotycin, Isopto PHN .5 and 1.5%, Isordil (also Sublingual and Tembids), Kenalog-S, Kryl Tab, MVI, Manibee (also C 500), Mannitol Hexanitrate, Maxitate, Metamine, Methyl Androstenediol, Meti-Derm and Neomycin, Metimyd (also with Meomycin), Metranil, Milpath (200 and 400), Mycolog (also 100,000 units), Myconef.

Neo-Aristocort, Neo-Aristoderm, Neo-Cort Dome (.5 and 1%), Neo-Cortef (.5, 1, 1.5 and 2.5%), Neo-Cortell, Neo-Decadron, Neo-Delta-

Cortef, Neo-Deltef, Neo-Deomeform-HC, Neo-Hydeltrasol, Neo-Hytone, Neo-Magnacort, Neo-Medrol (.25 and 1%), Neo-Nystra-Cort, Neo-Oxylone, Neo-Polycin HC, Neo-Resulin-F, Neo-Synlar, Neo-Tarcortin, Neodecadron, Neomycin Sul/HC (1 and 2.5%), Neomycin-HC (.5 and 1.%), Neosone, Neosporin (also G), Nilevar, Nitranitol, Nitretamin.

Predmycin P, Pro-Banthine with Phenobarbital, Proternol (30 mg.), Pyribenzamine Eph/Coex (also Eph^{c}Exp), Robinul-PH (also PH Fote), Soluzyme, Stendiol (25 and 50 mg/cc), Sufathalidine, Terra Cortril, Tetrasule-80, Theophorine Exp/Cod/Pap, Trasentine-Phenobarbital, Tuss-Ornade, Tussionex, Ulogesic, Ulominic, Vi Syneral (also 10 ML/vials), Vioform-HC Mild and with Hydrocortisone, Winsteroid, and Winstrol.

DRUGS DECLARED INEFFECTIVE BY FDA*
Di-ademil-K, Naturetin w/K (2.5, 5 mg.), Rautrax (also Rautrax Improved, -N, -N Modified) and Travamin/Dextrose.

DRUGS DECLARED INEFFECTIVE BY FDA*
Achrostatin V, Adrenosem Salicylate, Aerosporin, Alevaire, Ananase, Arlidin, Aureomycin Triple Sulfate, Avazyme, Azo Gantanol, Azotrex, Betadine, Biozyme Ointment, Butiserpazide (25 and 50), Butizide (25 and 50), Carbrital (also Carbrital Half Strength), Cartrax (10 and 20), Chymolase, Chymoral, Combid, Comycin, Cyclospasmol.

Deaner (25 and 100 mg.), Declostatin, Deprol, Dibenzyline, Diutensen, Duo-Medihaler, Equagesic, Equanitrate, (10 and 20), Eskatrol Spansules, Ilidar, Isordil with Phenobarbital, Lidosporin, Marax, Migral, Milprem (200 and 400 mg.), Miltrate, Mysteclin F (also-125 and V).

Octin, Onycho-Phytex, Orenzyme, Orthoxine, Otobione, Otobiotic, Oxaine, Oxsoralen, Papase, Pathilon, Pathilon/Phenobarbital, Paveril Phosphate, Peritrate w/Phenobarbital, PMB (200, 400), Polycline with Triple Sulfate), Potaba (0.5 and 2 gm.), Priscoline, Pro-Banthine with Dartal, Propion Gel.

Roniacol, Solusponge (Cone and Strip), Terrastatin, Tetrastatin, Tetrex Triple Sulfate, Tral Gradument, Trocinate, Vasodilan, Wilzyme, Wyanoids HC, Zactane, Zactirin.

*Source: *Help: 1980*
The Indispensable Almanac of Consumers Information
Everest House, New York

HEALTH INSURANCE

Sometimes I think insurance sellers will sell anything to make a buck. They make outrageous profits selling flight and cancer insurance at unfavorable odds. People buy it because they're scared.

Their hardest sell goes to policies that help you the least, because on those policies they make bigger commissions. Banks offer better deals on life insurance; so insurance company lobbyists pressure legislators to forbid banks to sell these policies.

Their policies are cleverly written in such complicated form it's nearly impossible to make price comparisons. Much of your policy money will never get back to you. It goes into overhead, fancy buildings, profits, and to paying squads of salespeople who go out to gyp other people.

On the other hand, a lot of us would be up the creek without insurance, and some of us ought to buy more of it than we have now.

Health insurance is one policy *everyone* should have. You can't afford not to have it. Getting sick is just too expensive— even a short hospital stay can wipe out years of savings.

Which policy should you buy? In general *group* policies offer the best deal. If your company offers a group health plan, grab it. If your company doesn't have a plan, try your church, or a club to which you belong. Group policies are almost always better than individual policies. They give you more coverage for less money.

If you can't join a group, you're faced with the horrible task of shopping for an individual policy. I say horrible because the policies are so complicated that thoroughly researching them would take years. A sample of the tricks:

With company #1, you're covered for sickness *manifested* after you sign up. With company #2, you're covered for sickness *contracted* after you sign up. The difference? Policy #1 is better. With policy #2, if you get cancer, company #2 might not cover you. "Yes, Mr. Sucker," says company #2, "we know doctors only discovered your cancer yesterday, and you've been paying us premiums for 10 years. But you probably *contracted* the cancer 15 years ago when you worked in that chemical plant. Since that was before you signed with us, you're not covered."

SOME GENERAL GUIDELINES

Get a policy that is "guaranteed renewable," not just "uncancelable." An "uncancelable" policy can be terminated whenever it expires. You could be left without insurance just when you need it most. The "guaranteed renewable" policy can never be canceled (although the premium may go up).

Don't buy mail-order policies. You'd think these would be good policies. Mail-order companies don't have to pay squads of salespeople. You'd think they'd use that money to pay more of your hospital bills. You'd think wrong. Mail-order policies tend to be bad deals.

Buy a Blue Cross/Blue Shield policy. They tend to be better than most.

Buy a policy from a company with a high pay-out rate. By pay-out, I mean the amount they pay out for every premium dollar they collect. In other words, a company with a 95% pay-out rate has been spending 95¢ of your dollar for policy holder's medical bills, and keeping only 5¢ for itself. That's a lot better than a company with a 50% pay-out rate. The 50% company probably has clever fine print in its contracts that enables it to keep 50¢ of each of your dollars. Pay-out rate isn't a perfect guide, but it's better than nothing. Here are the percentages for the biggest insurance companies:

COMPANY	PAY-OUT PERCENTAGE
Aetna Life	88.3
American Family Life Assurance, Georgia	48.9
American National	72.2
Bankers Life	74.0
Bankers Life and Casualty	66.5
Benefit Trust	86.8
Colonial Penn Life Insurance	62.9
Combined Insurance of America	43.4
Connecticut General Life	88.5
Continental Assurance	79.8
Equitable Life Assurance, New York	83.3
Fireman's Fund, California	77.2
General American	86.2
Group Life and Health	86.3
Guardian Life	76.2

Gulf Life Insurance	80.9
Hartford Life and Accident	77.7
Independent Life and Accident	41.8
John Hancock	83.9
Life Insurance Company of North America	79.1
Lincoln National	85.7
Massachusetts Mutual	83.5
Metropolitan Life	72.6
Metropolitan Property and Liability	117.4*
Mutual Benefit	72.4
Mutual of New York	77.9
Mutual of Omaha	75.9
National Home Life Assurance, Missouri	53.3
National Life and Accident	57.0
Nationwide Life	77.5
New England Mutual	72.9
New York Life	73.0
Occidental Life, California	90.2
Pacific Mutual	85.1
Paul Revere	70.6
Pennsylvania Life	48.7
Phoenix Mutual	79.4
Physicians Mutual	62.2
Pilot Life	89.9
Provident Life and Accident	82.6
Prudential Insurance Company of America	79.9
Republic National Life	83.8
State Mutual	77.5
Time Insurance	65.1
Travelers Insurance Company	88.3
Union Labor	86.4
Union Mutual Life	77.8
United Insurance Company of America	45.3
Wausau Life	81.7
Washington National	73.7

Source: 1979 Argus Health Chart—National Underwriter Company

*So this company lost money to its customers.

If a company you're considering is too small to be on this list, your state's insurance department will tell you the pay-out ratio of that company. Just call them up (under state listings—insurance, in the White Pages) and ask to talk to someone who handles health insurance.

FOR OLDER PEOPLE

If you are over 65, Medicare pays part of the your medical bills. Part. In recent years, the pay-out has averaged only 38%, so you still have to pay most of the bills yourself.

To pay the rest, the best thing to do is carry over the health insurance you had before you turned 65. However, some policies cannot be continued: you then may want to buy "medi-gap" coverage. It covers much of what Medicare doesn't cover. Lots of companies sell it. For example, it's a medi-gap policy that Art Linkletter keeps promoting in your Sunday paper.

Like most insurance policies, medi-gap policies vary widely in quality. Fortunately, the New York State Office for the Aging recently studied and rated these policies. Some rated far better than others. Linkletter's received only half as many rating points as some others. To get a copy of the ratings, send 67¢ in postage stamps to: Medi-gap, New York State Office for the Aging, Agency Building 2, Empire State Plaza, Albany, New York 12223.

CANCER INSURANCE—A POLICY YOU DON'T NEED

She answered the door and a nice-looking young man smiled at her and said, "Hi, I'm from the American Protection Company. I wonder if you have taken precautions, considering where you live?"

"What do you mean?" she asked.

"You know there have been an unusual number of cancer cases in this area." He pulled out a notebook. "We think it's because there's so much heavy industry up on the hill. Have your children been tested for cancer?"

She was crying when he left—afraid for her children—guilty for living where she lived. He was happy: he'd sold her a cancer insurance policy. The policy will pay her bills if cancer hospitalizes her for more than 91 days. The policy costs her $99 a year.

For selling it, the salesman got a fat $50 commission, and he'll get $9 per year after that. What? . . . $50 commission on a $99 policy? That leaves only $49 for the company's other employees, for profit, for building rental, paperwork, etc. Does that mean there's almost *nothing* left to pay out to policyholders stricken with cancer? It sure does.

Cancer insurance is a bad deal. Some states ban its sale altogether. It sells well because we are so scared of cancer (although heart disease is more likely to kill us). The companies selling it make phenomenal profits, because their cancer policies pay out very little relative to what they collect in premiums. They pay out little because the policies are cleverly worded to cover things that probably will never happen. For example, remember that policy that pays all hospital bills after 91 days? Well, that sounds good, but most cancer patients spend less than 15 days in the hospital; the heavy bills are away from the hospital (drugs, chemotherapy) and the policy cleverly excludes them.

Yes, you might get cancer and benefit from a cancer policy, but it's not likely. You are better off with general medical insurance. Even the American Cancer Society opposes cancer insurance.

DRINKING, GETTING DRUNK AND HANGOVERS

Alcohol makes you high because it acts as an anesthetic. You feel good because your nervous system has been partly shut off. For some reason, the part that shuts off first is the part that criticizes you and makes you tense. You relax. If you keep drinking, other parts shut off until you pass out.

How fast you get high depends on how fast the alcohol passes through the walls of your stomach and into your bloodstream. The blood brings the alcohol to your brain so it can begin doing its stuff. You can slow the process down by eating before you drink. Protein (milk, eggs, meat, nuts) slows the absorption of alcohol, so you get drunk more slowly. On the other hand, carbon dioxide speeds absorption, so carbonated drinks make you drunker faster.

Those times when you get sick drinking, it's probably because you drank too much too fast. Getting sick is your body's way of saying "no more!" It's a myth that mixing different types of drinks will make you drunker or sicker. Alcohol is alcohol. Your body doesn't care what kind of alcohol it is. However, when it comes to hangovers, your body does care about the kind of drink. That's because it's not just the alcohol that gives you the hangover, it's the congeners. Congeners are chemicals that form during the distilling process. They help give liquor its taste. The more congeners, the worse the hangover. Dark drinks like bourbon, Scotch, brandy, and red wine generally have more congeners than light drinks, like gin, vodka, and white wine. Therefore light-colored drinks will probably bring you less of a hangover.

Once you have the hangover, there's not much you can do. Drinking more will help, but only temporarily. When you stop, you'll have the hangover back, and worse. Your head aches because the alcohol has enlarged the blood vessels in your head. Aspirin helps. So will sitting up. Lying down is not a great idea. You just bring *more* blood to your head. Coffee or tea might help the headache because caffeine shrinks swollen blood vessels. So does an ice pack.

If your hangover symptom is an upset stomach, don't take aspirin. Aspirin can make an upset stomach worse. So don't take these products—Anacin, Excedrin, Bufferin, and Alka-Seltzer—because aspirin is the pain killer in them. You can take Alka-Seltzer Gold because it has no aspirin in it. You can take aspirin substitutes, like Tylenol and Datril; they won't upset your stomach.

If you're drunk, and want to sober up, you probably drink coffee. This won't work. Yes, it will help your headache later, but not your delirium now. Coffee just makes you a wide-awake drunk. A cold shower won't help you sober up either. If you want to sober up, the best thing you can do is sweat. Go dancing, run around the block, sit in a sauna, whatever. Sweating eliminates some of the alcohol through your skin before it gets a chance to work on your brain. Otherwise, you have to just sit it out.

Not everyone gets a hangover. Some people still seem fine the morning after a night on the town. Others, who may have had much less to drink, can't get out of bed. Recent research says people who feel most uptight about drinking are most likely to suffer later on. So, enjoy it. You'll feel better later.

Travel

If vacations are such fun, why do all these people write me such horrible letters? If you read my complaint mail, you'd never go anywhere. In fact, after I read it, I rented a summer house and now I go there instead of taking travel vacations.

There are more travel problems today because more people are traveling. The extra money attracts extra ripoff artists. Hotels are less grateful, more likely to take you for granted. Reading the following may help you spot the con-jobs and save you money.

FLYING

THE CHEAPEST FLIGHT

Taking a plane trip? There are dozens of fares. I won't bother trying to explain them (not that I could). Even if I did try, by the time you read this, the airlines probably would have changed the rules.

The fare system is hopelessly confusing. But that's not all bad; in fact, for us, it's good. Why care if you don't understand the fares? Airline employees don't understand them either. This means that if you play your cards right when booking a trip, you can fly for *less* than the lowest regular fare.

The trick is to call several airlines and ask for the lowest rate available. If your trip is the least bit complicated, I promise you that many clerks will give you different "lowest" fares. Why shouldn't they? The fare codes are so bizarre that you'd have to be a math expert to get them right. When you call, they're bound to make mistakes. I know. I've tried it.

I booked a flight from New York to London to Seattle and got fares ranging from $720 to $1,136. It was a zoo. One clerk said that the lowest legal fare was something like the "Left-Handed Chimpanzee Nightflight," while the next one patiently explained the "Chimpanzee Nightflight" is only good for cities with airports built after 1962, and what I wanted, he said, was the "Over-Arctic-Tuesday Excursion" fare, etc.

The result: I got several fares that turned out to be even cheaper than the lowest legal fare. And because they wrote the ticket that way, that's the way I could have flown.

Try it. It works.

BEING BUMPED

Airlines (hotels too) being no fools, book more seats (rooms) than they have. They know plenty of people make reservations and never show up. If they didn't overbook, every flight would be half empty; they'd lose bundles of money and the stockholders would throw them out on their ears. So they overbook, and once in while you happen to be on one of those flights where all the reservation holders actually show up and there are three hundred people trying to fit into a two-hundred-and-fifty-seat plane.

This can actually be a good thing. Play it right and the airline will pay you money *and* give you a free flight! Here's how to work it.

Current regulations require airlines to ask passengers on an overbooked flight, "Is anyone willing to get off and take a later flight, so passengers who cannot wait can get on? If you get off, we'll pay you X dollars." X averages $85 dollars, but will be higher if it's an expensive flight. If not enough people go for this bribe, the bumping begins. The usual policy is to bump the last people who arrive at the gate: last come, first bumped. If you are bumped, the airline must refund your ticket and put you on the next available flight. So, in effect, you *get a free ticket!*

Even better: If the airline cannot get you on another flight within 2 hours (4 hours on international flights), you not only get your ticket refunded and put on the next available flight, they'll also pay you the cost of the flight you take! You make out like a bandit. Free flight and free money.

So, the tricks: If you are in a hurry and can't handle being bumped, get there early. First come, last bumped.

If you've got time, and you're into legal gambling, arrive at the gate late. (But not too late. You may be ineligible for bumping benefits if you arrive less than 15 minutes before flight time.) If the flight is only slightly overbooked (ask the clerk) accept the $85 or so to get off. If it's very overbooked, or if it looks as though not enough people are taking the bribe, shut up, get bumped (because you arrived late) and take the free flight.

It's a matter of luck whether you get the flight *and* the money. Most times the airlines manages to get you on another plane within the 2-hour limit.

You may have to insist on your rights. The airlines don't have a great track record of telling bumpees what they are entitled to. You may have to go to the counter and say, "Hey, I want my free ticket."

You do *not* get the money or the free ticket if you were bumped for reasons other than overbooking. In other words, if the whole flight was canceled, or if the 747 had a flat tire and they had to change to a smaller plane, or (this one boggles the mind) if you were "removed to make room for a government official on emergency business," then you don't get bumping benefits.

However, any time you are inconvenienced, airlines give you stuff to keep you happy. You can get:

1. Food. If a flight is canceled and you have to hang around the airport during mealtime, most airlines will give you at least a greasy hamburger, if not an entire meal.
2. Room. If the delay goes overnight, they often provide free hotel rooms.
3. Talk. One long-distance phone call. To anywhere. But no more than 3 minutes.

When I tell people about these benefits they say, "What? The airline never gave *me* those things when my flight was canceled!" Airlines don't volunteer this information because it's expensive for them. It's also inconvenient. What if they give you a room, send you there, and then suddenly find they have a flight available for you? Delays are expensive. They'd rather have you hungry and sleepy, panting at the gate, ready to board. But the airline also wants to keep you happy. What's a $30 motel room to Airline A (it probably costs them less than $30 anyway), if it means a delighted passenger will buy future $300 cross-country tickets from Airline A instead of from nearly identical Airline B. So when you ask for the benefits, act prosperous. Mention your frequent flights to Paris.

"DIRECT" FLIGHTS

I was called by a Manhattan man who was furious because "I booked a flight from New York to St. Louis. They told me it was a direct flight, but we stopped in Detroit and Chicago. It's the pits, taking off and landing and waiting all the time. I want my money back! Or at least the airline's deception should be exposed!"

I can't help him. It's all in the terms. "Non-stop" flights don't stop. "Direct" flights can stop a zillion times. All "direct" means is that you don't change planes. I told him that. He sighed, swore and hung up.

LUGGAGE PROBLEMS

If the airline loses or mangles your luggage, it will probably pay you for it. Probably. Airlines aren't always cooperative about it. I can't really blame them, considering how many people cheat the airlines by filing phony claims.

It's up to you to prove you lost something (you may have to fight the airline in Small Claims Court, see page 201). Keep the baggage check. File the claim quickly (the law allows forty-five days, but sooner is better). Get the name of the clerk who helped you.

The most the airlines will pay for your bags is $750. If you are carrying something more valuable, you can buy extra insurance (10¢ for every $100 coverage). Expensive and fragile items, like musical instruments or antiques, they may not insure. Ask the ticket clerk.

WHICH AIRLINE FOR YOU?

Assuming you are not a TV reporter, this chart may be helpful. It lists the least and most complained about airlines. Note the list gives complaints per 100,000 passengers, so it doesn't favor smaller airlines.

I get good service on all airlines. I have never been bumped, never lost a bag, never suffered any horrible delays. Maybe it's because I'm a TV consumer reporter and they see me coming.

COMPLAINTS* PER 100,000 PASSENGERS

AIRLINE	AUGUST 1977–AUGUST 1979
DELTA	1.75
UNITED	4.52
WESTERN	5.00
EASTERN	5.18
CONTINENTAL	5.44
AMERICAN	6.36
NORTHWEST	7.85
BRANIFF	8.10
TWA	8.10
NATIONAL	9.35
PAN AMERICAN	11.21

*COMPLAINTS TO THE CIVIL AERONAUTICS BOARD.

It's not a perfect guide; no one checks to see if the complaints are valid. Delta stands apart from the field as the least complained about airline. On the opposite end, people complain consistently more about Braniff, TWA, National and Pan American. National and Pan Am may have merged by the time you read this. I hope they don't lay off any of their complaint staffs.

AIRLINE COMPLAINTS

If you have problems, there are three complaint procedures. I recommend the first:

1. Yell and scream. Embarrass people. Airlines are very concerned about maintaining dignity. They don't want unruly

customers. If you don't want to make a scene, simply stand at the counter and firmly insist on your rights. Quietly but clearly. Repeat yourself like a broken record. They'll come around.

2. Write the airline. Get the name of the person who helped (or didn't help) you.

3. Write the Civil Aeronautics Board, Washington, D.C., 20408. The CAB is the agency that deals with any type of airline complaint. They will (a) intervene with the airline and pressure them to give you your due, or (b) decide you are a nut and junk your complaint, or (c) lose your letter.

FLIGHT INSURANCE

This is a bad deal. Insurance companies make a fortune on flight insurance.

Yes, leaving the ground in a hollow metal tube seems life-threatening, but statistically, you are twice as likely to die riding a bicycle.

To protect your family in case you die, buy regular term life insurance. Flight insurance is a ripoff.

GETTING BY CUSTOMS

You know the rules: Up to $300 in merchandise—no duty. Over $300 you pay 12% to 22% tax. Paying the tax may be worth it; many things are more than 22% cheaper abroad. But if you don't declare it, and they catch you, you pay a fine of up to six times normal duty.

Tip: Customs inspectors tell me the maximum fine is reserved for travelers who intentionally cheat. If you convince them you were simply ignorant of the rules, they fine you less.

Tip: If they catch you with something undeclared, they'll ask, "Is that all?" If you confess then, the fine is cheaper than if they catch you with more. And as one inspector puts it: "Once we catch you with something, we search harder."

Don't bring food home. Customs inspectors will confiscate it. The scenes are incredible. People fight for their food. I watched a tug-of-war over an Italian sausage. Literally, a tug-of-war. The woman started to cry. She accused the customs inspector of taking the food for himself.

In truth, most international airports have giant garbage disposals that eat confiscated food. The one at Kennedy Airport is the size of a small car. I watched it grind up hundreds of oranges, assorted other fruits, sugar cane, milk from Israel, a whole standing rib roast from Brazil. It all goes into the sewers. This is supposed to prevent exotic diseases from sneaking into the country.

It's necessary. The last disease that sneaked in was Newcastle disease. One imported parakeet brought it into the country. American chickens caught it. Eleven million of them had to be killed. It cost the United States $25,000,000.

BY TRAIN OR BUS

Not much to say about this, except that the prices are often strange. The bus is usually cheaper than the train, the train cheaper than the plane, but not always. For example, from New York to Los Angeles, it's cheaper to fly than to ride the train.

1979 PRICE SAMPLES:
New York–Los Angeles
Plane: $144 (discount fare)
Amtrak: $206
Greyhound: $95

New York–Washington, D.C.
Plane: $56
Amtrak: $27
Greyhound: $25

THE PACKAGE TRIP

Those too-good-to-be-true advertisements ($359 for 7 days in Peru), are not necessarily ripoffs. Package deals are the cheapest way to travel. Airlines and hotels discount heavily when they are assured of getting a big group.

But there are plenty of traps. Take the following ad:

SEE SUNNY MEXICO!
FROM $199*

Superior Hotel

Pool

Color TV

Great Location

For Your Convenience:
  Flights leave August 3, 8, 9, 18
  September 9, 12, 28
  October 1, 3, 10, 29

TRANS AM-AIRWAYS/BIG TIME TRAVEL CO.

*includes welcome cocktail, historical tour, free reading
material, wildlife safari

Travel ads are often total phonies. Who will prosecute a Mexican
hotel for lying in a brochure? Your local district attorney? Even
without lying, ads can be deceptive. The ad on this page has no
direct lies. Yet:

> SUPERIOR HOTEL—"Superior" is generally meaningless.
> Even when ratings count, superior can be the third rating,
> below luxury and deluxe.
> POOL—To be built. Soon.
> COLOR TV—In the manager's office, not in the rooms.
> GREAT LOCATION—Great for whom? The stories roll in about
> beach hotels miles from the beach.

The picture of the ocean may indeed have been taken in Mexico, though nowhere near your hotel. Sometimes ad agencies use the same pictures for different hotels.

"Friday sightseeing downtown" may be two hours' sightseeing after five hours on the bus from an out-of-the-way hotel. I suggest you go to the library and look up the hotel in a travel book. *Hotel Redbook, Fielding's Favorites,* and *Fodor* and *Michelin* guides are good. CHECK THE LOCATION; it may not be where the ad implies it is. If you buy a Fielding guidebook, you get an extra service: a toll-free telephone number you can call seven days a week for up-to-date travel information. They'll tell you current exchange rates, late changes in prices, weather predictions, political warnings, availability of gasoline, etc., for most European countries.

FLIGHTS LEAVE AUGUST . . . 3, 8, 9, 18; SEPTEMBER . . . 9, 12, 28; OCTOBER . . . 1, 3, 10, 29—*Travel Promoter:* "Sure they will, if I can find enough travelers to fill each of those planes. I probably can't, so I'll cancel 18 out of 20 flights, and everyone will have to go on those days. Sure, they'll have to scramble to adjust their vacations, but if I didn't list all those choices, they would probably never have signed up."

Fewer than half the charter flights registered with the CAB get off the ground. Most charters never fly.

FROM $199 *—Note the "From"; $199 may be the price only on Thursday, October 3rd.

Note the asterisk in the ad. The items listed after * are offered to any tourist, package plan or not. "Reading material" is the Bible in the hotel room. "Wildlife" means the insects that creep through the hotel.

TRANS-AM AIRWAYS/BIG TIME TRAVEL—Yes, the flight is on a real airplane, owned by an established airline. Yes, the package is sold through BIG TIME and several reputable travel agencies. But the real tour operator is Fly-by-Night Travel Wholesaler, and if you look at the fine print on the contract, you'll see that TRANS-AM and BIG TIME assume no legal responsibility for your trip.

Moral: Go where your friends have gone and liked it. If your friends never go anywhere, ask the travel agent for names of people who did go. Call them up. You might even make friends.

Observe that of all the treats listed under*, airfare is not one of them. This is a common trick, designed to lure you into the travel agency. Once there, all excited about the trip, you pay the extra money.

One woman called me, in tears: "I just had to cancel my vacation. The travel brochure never said airfare wasn't included. They only told me at the last second." In this case, the advertisement didn't even have an asterisk. It implied airfare was included. It sounded like intentional deception to me, so I went to the wholesaler, accompanied by a WCBS-TV crew, cameras rolling.

Stossel: I've received complaints about your Guadeloupe trip.
Manager: I'm not interested in discussing it. Is that clear?
Stossel: We're going on television with what people have said about you.
       We'd like to give you a chance to rebut . . .
Manager: Would you like me to call the police?

We left. I have no right, after all, to film on his property if he tells me to leave.

The state attorney general said, "Yes, the wholesaler's ad is deceptive." There was never any prosecution, however. Not enough complaints. This wholesaler, according to the Better Business Bureau, has been running deceptive ads for years. After we put him on TV, he stopped.

TRAVEL AGENTS

You might as well go to one. It costs you nothing since agents are paid by the airlines and hotels.

I have no firm guidelines for finding a good agent. Some agents belong to trade groups like the American Society of Travel Agents (ASTA) and display the ASTA sticker in their windows as if it were a guarantee of honesty or expertise. It's not.

Some agents give you help that's worse than no help at all. One customer came back with this complaint. "I arrived in Caracas to find the hotel knew nothing of my prepayment. The agency apparently had never forwarded it. The hotel was full and I had to stay in a dump out of town. Then at the airport, when I gave them my return flight ticket, the airline clerks laughed. They said there was no such fare and the ticket was improperly written. I had to borrow money from a friend to pay the extra money to get home."

Remember, some agents are kids who take the job to get free trips, or retired people who use the job as a way to make their travels tax-deductible. On the other hand, there are those agents who take pride in being experts. They travel a lot, and advise people only about areas they are familiar with. Remember, no agent can be an expert on every vacation spot. Shop around.

SPECIAL BARGAINS

If you are a student, there are discounts all over the world. But, you've got to prove that you're a student. Send $2.50 to the Council of International Educational Exchange, 777 UN Plaza, New York, New York 10017 (212-MO 1-0310). Enclose a passport-size photo, and a student ID card (or your grades, or disciplinary probation, or something to prove that you are a student). The Association will give you a student ID card that is recognized internationally.

CHEAP "HOTELS"

Student or not, it's dirt cheap, if you are traveling in the U.S., to overnight on a college campus. Schools are picking up extra money renting rooms. The Hotel-Motel Association is furious about it, saying it's unfair, tax-free competition. They have a point, but at the moment it's legal and wonderfully cheap. For example:

- Coe College (Iowa): single room for $7 per day. Tennis and swimming are free. Bicycles, volleyball and racquet ball equipment are available, free.

- University of Maine: Want to visit the Maine woods? Stay here a *week* for $35.
- Washington University (St. Louis): Rooms—$6 per day. Outdoor tennis and indoor swimming, free.

These are only samples. For the complete guide, send $5 to CMG Publishing Co., P.O. Box 630, Princeton, New Jersey 08540. Ask for *Low Cost Vacations & Lodgings on Campuses.*

FREE VACATION HOMES

Home-swapping is such a bargain, I'm amazed that it's not better known. Imagine going to Haiti, staying in a luxurious villa . . . three servants . . . a chauffeur-driven car. Too expensive? After you pay the airfare, as long as you're willing to offer your home or apartment in return, it's all free. So is two weeks at a California beach house or three weeks in an Oregon ski house.

If you are interested, you can find offers like that in a directory published by a home-swapping club. It works this way: you pay the club a fee of $15 or more. They print your name and a description of your home in their directory. You may also list your vacation preference. For example:

John Doe, 10 E. 4th St., New York City. 4-room apartment near Greenwich Village. I prefer to go to the sun in December or January.

"Fantastic . . ." "Wonderful every time . . ." "I can't believe we didn't do this before . . ." These are comments I've heard from home-swappers. People often prefer to live in homes instead of hotels. Sometimes, the homeowners arrange parties so you get to meet the neighbors.

The listings are circulated among club members. Then you call each other to try to arrange swaps. (Sample listings follow.) You vacation in their house. They stay in yours. A good deal for everyone.

OKLAHOMA

Mr./Mrs. BRYCE MOORE, 2301 W. Tecumseh St., Tulsa 74127—3 bdrm hse, 2 ad (adults), exch or rnt @500/mo, anytime, no pf; a-c, views, fireplace, woodlands, pools, tennis, horses, bicycling, close to downtown, university, quiet nbhd, retired USAF (Col.).

PATRICIA BRATRUDE, 3333 E. 38, Apt. 12, Tulsa 74135—2 bdrm/2 bth apt, 2 ad, exch or rnt @325/mo plus elec, anytime, no pf; fireplace, bar, pool, no ch (children) or pets, prefer single non-smokers or drinkers, nr lakes, occupation: retired gov't.

OREGON

JOAN M. MORGAN, 318 North Shore Rd., Lake Oswego 97034—3-4 bdrm hse, 1 ad, exch or rnt, anytime, pf: USA, M, LA, PAC, anywhere; warm, exotic den, fireplace, dining room, piano, lake view, 1 block to swim and boat, corner fenced yard, ocean & mtn nearby, cat, teacher.

LYLE H. GRAMS, Rt. #1 Box 136A, Yoncalla 94799—2 bdrm hse. 2 ad, exch, anytime (retired), no pf; new home on hillside, view, 1 hr from ocean, mountains, near rivers, central western Oregon.

Mr./Mrs. DUANE F. SMITH, P.O. Box 962, Ashland 97520—3 bdrm hse, 2 ad/2 ch, exch, *May-Aug, pf: Germany; 2 baths, sauna, fantastic view, a-c, Shakespeare Theatre, close to town, occupation: investments.

Mr./Mrs. RICHARD YODER, 2105 Haworth Ave., Newberg 97132—2 bdrm condominium apt at Sunriver, 2 ad/3 ch, exch or rnt @240—300/ wk, *23/June-5/July, pf: Eur,M,PAC, anywhere; yr-round resort, view, golf, tennis, pools, bicycling, fishing, skiing, ice skating, color TV, tech rep.

Mr./Mrs. MIKE BERGSTROM, 2115 NE Hwy 20, Corvallis 97330—3 bdrm hse at Lebanon, 2 ad/2 ch, exch, *1/Jan-1/Mar, pf. Eur,M,PAC; golf course lot, 3 stories, secluded, fireplace, huge jacuzzi bath, dishwasher, car, skiing, golfing, fishing close.

STEWART E. MAYO, 1211 Scenic View Ct., Stayton 97383—3 bdrm hse, 2 ad, exch or rnt @300/mo, *Nov-May, pf: Eur,M,PAC, anywhere; near state capital and Portland, valley view, extra bath, decks, a-c, 2 cars, food chemist.

Source: Vacation Exchange Club Directory.

I've heard no complaints about homes badly damaged by guests (though it's bound to happen eventually; check your insurance). Everyone I talked to was delighted with their swapping experience. You certainly can't beat the price.

The following are three home-swapping clubs and their 1979 prices for listing and subscription to the Annual Directory. "Arrangements" means that if you pay the extra money, the club arranges the swap for you. Then you don't have to write letters to the potential swapees.

CLUB	COST	ARRANGEMENTS
Vacation Exchange Club 350 Broadway New York, N.Y. 10013	$15 Photo $5 extra	None
Iniquiline, Inc. 35 Adams Street Bedford Hills, N.Y. 10507	$50 Photo included	$100
Interchange Home Exchange 888 Seventh Avenue New York, N.Y. 10019	$12 Photo included	$110

TRAVELERS CHEQUES

No argument here; if you travel, buy some. If the checks are lost or stolen, the check companies really will refund your money, usually without giving you a hard time. Usually.

Watch for tricky thieves. If your check packet is stolen, you would, of course, report it; and the thief might be caught trying to cash the checks. But today's alert burglar steals maybe three of twenty checks, replaces the packet and you don't notice the checks missing. To catch this, be sure to flip through the packet now and then and note the number sequence.

Financially, checks are a bad buy. You lend the bank money at no interest; they use your money until you spend the checks. On top of that, most banks charge a 1% sales fee. Some don't, including Barclays. But before you rush to Barclays, listen to what happened to Cliff Katz.

Katz called me looking for help. "I'm pawning my guitar and my ring," he said. "Barclays won't pay me for my (lost) travelers cheques." Katz told a strange story. A year ago, he cashed in all his savings and bought travelers cheques from Barclays—

$60,000 worth. He was going to travel on business for a year visiting many countries, and he wanted ready money. He spent $30,000 of the checks, returned to the U.S., and was promptly robbed of the rest. He went to Barclays and asked for a refund. Barclays gave him $750.

"What about the rest?" asked Katz. "No, not yet," said a Barclays executive. "We have to check it out first." Katz kept asking for his money. Weeks passed. He pawned his possessions. It made for wonderful newsfilm, Katz pawning his last goods over Christmas, in the snow yet!

I called Barclays, posing as a customer.

Stossel: If the cheques are stolen, I get a refund?
Barclays: Even if you lose thousands in cheques, you get a total refund within, at most, four days.

So next time Katz went to Barclays, I followed with a camera crew. No Barclays official would speak with me. A few days later, they paid Katz the full $30,000. The New York State Banking Department says it's not unusual for a bank to stall on travelers cheques refunds. If fraud is involved, it gives them more time to see if someone is cashing the stolen checks. Katz's large loss certainly gave Barclays the right to be suspicious. But why couldn't they explain that to him? Or give him more than $750 while they investigated?

RENTING A CAR

The rates are impossible to understand. There are "dry" rates, weekend rates, "wet" rates, business rates, and so on . . . So, do what we did with the airlines (see page 156); call several companies and take the cheapest price. It may be the wrong price, but that's their problem, not yours.

The New York City Department of Consumer Affairs tried this with eleven rental companies. They found each company giving different "lowest" prices almost every time they called. On a one-day, 100-mile, compact-car rental, Budget quoted "lowest" prices from $19.95 to $54. Avis quoted from $47 to $66. Quite a difference.

Warning: If you don't have a credit card, some car rental companies require a deposit before they'll give you the car. Ask how much. It may be as high as $200. Also, some companies will not accept cash. You must pay by credit card or no deal.

MISCELLANEOUS TIPS

If you are worried about getting sick, and nervous about foreign doctors, MEDICAL ASSISTANCE FOR TRAVELERS will give you a list of English-speaking doctors who are in the area you'll be visiting. Get the names by writing to MEDICAL ASSISTANCE FOR TRAVELERS, 350 Fifth Avenue, Suite 5620, New York, New York 10001.

When changing money or cashing travelers cheques, you'll find exchange rates are generally better at banks than at your hotel.

Keep a close eye on your luggage. There is a new gimmick for making off with your bags. The thief puts a bottomless suitcase on top of your luggage. The device clamps shut. The thief walks right by you, with your bag hidden inside the trick suitcase.

If you travel a lot, I suggest you subscribe to *Travel Smart*. It's an excellent newsletter that will alert you to flight bargains . . . problems at certain vacation spots . . . and undiscovered resorts. To subscribe, write Communications House, Dobbs Ferry, New York 10522.

Financial Planning

Much of this chapter concerns subjects we don't like to think about. Better think about them anyway. Not thinking about them costs you lots of money.

LIFE INSURANCE

You've certainly got to have life insurance if you have loved ones dependent on your income. But how much? There are so many variables:

Will your children have to make mortgage payments on your house? For how long?

Do you want to guarantee their college costs?

Can your spouse go to work and make up for your loss of income?

The list is endless. You need to sit down and figure out what it costs to support your family, year by year. Add it up, subtract your savings from that, and that's the insurance you need.

Don't worry about figuring inflation. Yes, everything will cost more later, but your family will invest the insurance settlement, won't they? The interest on the investment should just about equal inflation.

If you don't have any dependents, I wouldn't buy any life insurance. Some insurance broker may try to convince you to buy as an investment, to protect yourself against a future when you may have dependents ("At that time, Mr./Ms. Jones, you'll be older, and life insurance will be more expensive"). Throw the guy out. True, life insurance will be more expensive later, but so what? It's still smarter to buy only when you actually need the protection. As for the investment part, life insurance is a lousy investment. A Federal Trade Commission report says insurance policies that offer "savings" paid a return of only 1.3% in 1977. The return is better now, but still less than what you can get on a savings account.

When you do buy, buy *term* insurance. Term insurance insures you for a specific period of time (the "term"). You pay a premium every year. If you die, your family collects. If you don't die, you're out the premium. No tricks, no gimmicks, just straightforward insurance. The life insurance salesperson, however, will try to sell you whole life, or "cash value," or "straight life" insurance—the reason being they make a bigger commission on those policies. Ignore it. Buy "term." Whole life insurance gives you far less protection for every dollar you spend. The salesperson will babble about Whole life's "savings value" and how it will "pay you when you're 65 even if you don't die." Maybe it will, but it's still a poor investment (that's the one that returns 1.3%).

Policy costs vary, so it pays to call several companies. The more expensive the policy, remember, the more incentive the agent has to sell it. If you're too lazy to comparison shop, at least don't pay more than the price quoted on the following charts. If you do, I think you are being ripped off.

Notice that some policies cost hundreds of dollars more than others. It pays to shop around.

Some of Connecticut Mutual's rates are high, but they give you some of the money back in dividends. All companies with Mutual in their name pay dividends.

If possible, buy your life insurance from a bank, instead of an insurance company. Banks give you much more insurance for the same premium. Unfortunately, in most states, insurance-company lobbyists have pressured legislators into passing laws that forbid banks to sell life insurance. At this writing, banks sell life insurance only in New York, Connecticut and Massachusetts.

It's a shame. In legislatures, insurance-money talks.

ONE YEAR RATES—TERM INSURANCE

FEMALE

Age	AETNA $25,000	$100,000	$200,000	BENEFICIAL NATIONAL LIFE $25,000	$100,000	$200,000	CONNECTICUT GENERAL $25,000	$100,000	$200,000	CONNECTICUT MUTUAL $25,000	$100,000	$200,000
20	$ 93.25	$ 197	$ 379	$ 48.75	$ 173	$ 346	$ 72.50	$ 230	$ 440	$ 81	$ 164	$ 298
25	94.25	199	383	51.25	178	356	73.75	235	450	81	156	282
30	96.00	210	405	56.50	189	378	76.25	245	470	81	183	336
35	99.50	226	437	66.00	196	392	82.00	268	516	87	202	374
40	109.00	255	495	86.25	225	450	97.00	328	636	102	250	470
45	145.25	345	675	129.25	327	654	121.25	425	830	128	323	616
50	205.25	503	991	193.50	500	1,000	164.00	596	1,172	169	447	864
55	294.00	760	1,505	273.75	779	1,558	246.50	926	1,832	258	679	1,328
60	421.50	1,246	2,477	457.25	1,224	2,448	—	—	—	378	1115	2,200

Life insurance for women is a little cheaper because women live longer

ONE YEAR RATES—TERM INSURANCE

MALE

Age	AETNA $25,000	$100,000	$200,000	BENEFICIAL NATIONAL LIFE $25,000	$100,000	$200,000	CONNECTICUT GENERAL $25,000	$100,000	$200,000	CONNECTICUT MUTUAL $25,000	$100,000	$200,000
20	$ 93.75	$ 198	$ 381	$ 50.25	$ 174	$ 348	$ 73.50	$ 234	$ 448	$ 92	$ 227	$ 424
25	95.00	207	399	52.75	186	372	76.00	244	468	92	199	368
30	98.00	219	423	57.75	194	388	79.00	256	492	92	202	374
35	102.75	243	471	74.25	202	404	85.50	282	544	97	231	432
40	127.75	318	621	109.25	279	558	108.00	372	724	122	322	614
45	177.75	457	899	167.50	421	842	151.75	547	1,074	172	479	928
50	256.50	684	1,353	253.00	652	1,304	214.25	797	1,574	247	710	1,390
55	364.00	1,057	2,099	359.00	1,025	2,050	324.75	1,239	2,458	377	1,058	2,086
60	544.00	1,629	3,243	638.00	1,640	3,280	500.50	1,942	3,864	581	1,648	3,266

FUNERALS

Here's a subject no one likes to think about. But if you deal with it now, before you or someone in your family dies, you're far better off than if you try to handle it at the moment of death.

A fancy funeral sometimes makes people feel better. Arranging it may make you feel you have done your duty to a loved one. The ceremony sometimes helps people accept that the person is really gone, and they are better able to go on with their own lives. So you may *want* to pay for a fancy funeral. But you don't *have* to.

I've heard many sad tales about grieving families who've been coaxed into spending more than they can afford to bury a loved one.

When a family member dies, most people are too upset to quibble about prices. Dishonest funeral directors have been taking advantage of this for years. You can be buried for $500, yet the average funeral cost $2,300. If you don't want to pay more than necessary, here are ripoffs to look for:

"You must have a casket for cremation." It's not required.

"The law says the body must be embalmed." It doesn't.

"The cheapest casket here is $500." Many funeral homes put their cheapest wooden casket ($100) in another room, so ask for it.

For more information, call a Memorial Society. These non-profit groups help people plan inexpensive funerals. The Continental Association of Funeral and Memorial Societies (1828 L Street, N.W., Washington, D.C. 20036) will tell you how to contact a Memorial Society near you.

There are alternatives to the $2,000 funeral:

A simple burial. There is a short ceremony by the grave. The body is buried in a simple wooden casket. The cost is about $500 ($200 if you do not wish any ceremony).

Cremation. The funeral director picks up the body, and takes it to the crematory, where it is burned, then brings the ashes to the family and fills out the necessary forms. A few days later, a memorial service may be held. Cost: $225 to $475, depending on how much traveling the funeral director must do. If there is viewing before cremation, the cost may be $500 to $900. That includes embalming the body for viewing.

Donating your body to science. A Memorial Society will tell you how to go about it; you could also call the anatomy department of a local medical school. Cost: A funeral director might charge about $100 to deliver the body. Some medical schools need bodies so badly they will come to pick it up, free.

TAXES

Most every April, I go to IRS headquarters and interview the clerks about whom they plan to audit, and what weird things people try to deduct.

Bob O'Connell, IRS: "Usually it's animals, they'll claim their cat as an exemption . . . horses . . . they'll claim fish . . ."

Stossel: "What do they say when you tell them 'You can't deduct that?'"

O'Connell: "They say . . . 'It's part of the family . . . why can't I get the deduction?'"

Abe Kern, IRS: "One time I got a dead fish in the envelope . . . with a rude note . . . what we could do with the fish . . ."

The most useful thing I've learned from my trips to the IRS is that the whole thing is a kind of game. I used to think it was scary. The idea of an audit terrified me. Now I know what the tax accountants understood all along: Unless you overtly cheat, nothing too serious is going to happen to you. Fewer than 1 in 3,000 people audited go to jail. Those that do go to jail have done something pretty flagrant, and probably have been turned in by informers. Informers get 10% of whatever the IRS recovers from the informee (that's something to think about next time you're bragging about how you cheated on your income tax). Those who go to jail usually have lied about *income*. If you're honest about reporting your income, there's almost no chance you'll go to jail. People who can't prove all their deductions are merely asked to pay what they owe, plus interest. Sometimes you have to pay a penalty, but not often.

AVOIDING THE AUDIT

There's no foolproof protection, because some returns are audited at random. Also, you reduce the chance of an audit by making less money, and that's hardly a worthwhile ambition. These points aside, your best bet is to claim those deductions the IRS considers "average" or "usual." The computer is programmed to spit out "unusual" returns, because over the years the IRS found that the people who file them are more likely to be cheaters.

So what is average? The following chart shows the average medical, charitable, interest, and tax deductions for different income brackets:

Adjusted Gross Income	Charitable Contributions	Interest	Taxes	Medical & Dental
$ 8000–10,000	$ 524	$1,507	$1,147	$1,100
10,000–12,000	527	1,589	1,179	882
12,000–14,000	475	1,706	1,242	806
14,000–16,000	479	1,868	1,421	669
16,000–18,000	559	1,880	1,553	670
18,000–20,000	532	2,006	1,720	596
20,000–25,000	563	2,085	1,954	505
25,000–30,000	676	2,271	2,300	520
30,000–50,000	893	2,637	3,124	551
50,000–100,000	1,965	4,230	5,488	748
100,000 +	9,673	9,345	13,839	1,063

Source: Consumers' Clearing House, Chicago

A big casualty loss may bring you an audit. The average loss is $607. If you have a bigger loss, include proof. In other words, if your house is hit by a tornado, include a picture and an appraisal. The computer may spit your return out, but then it goes to an actual human being, who can call the audit off if you convince the auditor a tornado really did hit your house.

Okay. Suppose you do receive that wonderful letter. "Dear taxpayer: we are examining your tax return, and find we need additional information to verify your correct tax. We have scheduled the above appointment for you." Now what?

First, you should realize that you have some flexibility. You can call the department up and reschedule the appointment. You can ask what it's about, and what records to bring. You can negotiate; the auditor is not a machine. They're only trying to recover as much money as possible with the least effort. If you're wrong, if you don't have the records to support your deductions, they'll simply tell you so, and state what you have to pay. If you're right, fight. Don't give in. If the auditor is being unreasonable, you can appeal, and you don't need a lawyer.

Not all audits end badly for the taxpayer. In 1 out of 4 cases, the IRS finds nothing wrong. In 6% of the audits, the IRS finds a mistake *in your favor*.

TAX CONSULTANTS

Do you do-it-yourself or get professional help? I believe in getting help. That's why I haven't listed zillions of individual tips. I used to do my own taxes; I thought I was getting all the deductions I deserved. Then I went to a tax accountant and he found plenty of things I had overlooked. He saved me enough to pay his fee, and then some.

Who should you go to? I once had the IRS prepare a phony tax identity for me. They gave me W-2 forms, two jobs, medical bills, charitable deductions, and a mother I support but could not legally claim as a dependent. The IRS said that under these conditions I owed the government $1,119 in federal tax.

Then, accompanied by a hidden camera, I went to H & R Block and had them prepare tax forms for my phony identity. The Block agent charged me $40 and said I owed the IRS only $558. I went to another H&R Block office. There they said I owed $460. At least H&R Block goofed in *my* favor. I then went to one of the IRS's own Help Centers. Help Centers say they will only answer specific questions, but in fact they just about prepare the return for you. The Help Center man said I owed the government $2,160! Afterwards I questioned the Help Center supervisor:

(The following is an abridged transcript of a report broadcast on WCBS-TV News.)

Stossel: "We took this return that you helped us prepare to one of your Help Centers, and they had us paying almost twice the tax you said we should pay."

Robert Carroll, IRS Taxpayer Services Division: "Well, this is unfortunate, John, but sometimes mistakes are made, even by independent accounting firms. It has to do with the complexity of the tax law."

I've surveyed tax consultants several times and gotten a different result from each tax preparer *every time*. The problem with H&R Block is that the preparer is paid *per return,* so the less time spent on you, the more money the preparer makes. On the other hand, you know H&R Block will be there should you get audited. Some tax preparers disappear after tax time.

You might get better results going to a Certified Public Accountant. CPAs must pass tax tests. An IRS survey found CPAs make fewer mistakes preparing taxes. On the other hand, CPAs cost more ($100 is typical). I think they are worth it.

IRAs AND KEOGH PLANS

If you are self-employed or work for a company with no pension plan, Keoghs and IRAs are excellent ways to shelter a little money from the tax collector. You get to put away a percentage of your income for retirement, and you don't pay tax on it until you are 65 (if you withdraw the money before you are 65 you must pay a penalty).

Banks, mutual funds, and insurance companies sell these plans. Buy one from a bank or mutual fund. *Never* buy one from an insurance company. I interviewed one man who'd deposited $1,200 in his insurance-company Keogh. One day he decided he needed the money and asked to withdraw everything from his account. "There is nothing in your account," said the insurance agent. "All the money has gone to company fees and commissions." I investigated and found this to be true. In later years the fees would have been lower, but for the first year, the insurance company had eaten his entire deposit. Legally. Most insurance companies operate this way. Banks and mutual funds usually don't take such fat commissions.

CHARITY

One way to keep your money from the IRS is to give it to charity. Not all charities are equally charitable, however. Considering what some do with your money, you might prefer giving it to the IRS.

Once in a while I collect for charity. It's not too difficult. Last time I got $16 in ten minutes. At the rate I was going, I would have amassed $800 by the end of the day. All I had to do was stand in front of Rockefeller Center screaming, "National Cancer Society!" Nobody who contributed bothered to check if their donations would actually go for medical care or if I was keeping it for myself!

It's heartwarming the way people drop money in the can without asking me whether there *is* such a thing as the National Cancer Society. There isn't; I made it up. Because I'm a decent person (of course, being recorded for television had nothing to do with it), I didn't keep the money. I told each donator I was a phony, and explained that they were going to be on *The Six O'Clock News*. They usually stared at me uncomprehendingly, then shrugged and walked off. Nobody's hit me yet.

The point of making a fool of people in front of a large TV audience is to illustrate how easily we give to charities without questioning their validity.

Checking charities out is very easy. All you have to do is write the National Information Bureau, 419 Park Avenue South, New York, New York 10016 or the Council of Better Business Bureaus, 1150 17th St. N.W. Washington, D.C. 20036. They'll give you detailed reports on any three charities you ask about . . . free.

Some charities give 60¢ of your dollar to the needy, and keep 40¢ for salaries, office furnishings, and fund-raising expenses. Better charities keep overhead down and give 80¢ of your dollar to the needy. The N.I.B. and C.B.B.B. will tell you which charity does which. They might even tell you the charity you've supported for years uses most of your donation to pay for the boss's Caribbean trips.

Here are two of my favorite charity ripoffs:

1. Two sturdy-looking men, wearing blue uniforms and badges, come to your door collecting for the Police Relief Fund or another official-sounding organization. Beware. They're probably not real cops. They'll just take your money and run. Many people give, because they feel intimidated by seeing police at their door (Why? Have you done something wrong lately?). Most legitimate charities don't solicit door-to-door. If an official type comes, ask to see the badge. That's still not foolproof; phonies often carry phony badges.

2. Last Christmas I wondered if the Santa Clauses collecting downtown were really giving their receipts to the poor. The answer? Not really, Virginia. Most of the Santas turned out to be collecting for Hare Krishna. Hare Krishna members dress up in red suits and make thousands of dollars each season. I brought a camera crew over:

(The following is an abridged transcript of a report broadcast on WCBS-TV News.)

Stossel: "Don't you think it's deceptive what you're doing?"

Gadhadahr Pandit, Secretary, Hare Krishna Society: "Well, when you look at Santa, hopefully you should think of God, because the spirit of Christmas and Santa Claus is the spirit of giving and helping others. That's not restricted to any one group or any one religion. The love of God is something for all people."

Traditionally, the Santas in my area were people collecting for the Volunteers of America. They still collect, but now they are outnumbered by the Hare Krishna Santas. The Volunteers of America give the money to needy families. The Krishna give some money to the poor, but most of the collection goes to promote the Hare Krishna.

Later on I interviewed people who gave to the Hare Krishna Santas:

Stossel: "Hello, I'm from WCBS. Do you know you just gave to a Hare Krishna Santa?"

Woman in Street: "Don't tell me that!"
Stossel: "Yes, he's a Hare Krishna."
Woman: "&%#$%!!"
Stossel: "They say they tell everyone they're Hare Krishna."
Woman: "He most certainly did not. He gave out candy canes, and that's the only reason I stopped. I feel sick."

MAKING MONEY ON THE SIDE

At times we all need a little more money and not just to give to charity. Here are some thoughts on how you might earn a little more.

SELLING GARBAGE

A few states now have laws requiring that all cans and bottles be returnable for deposit. This cuts litter and saves the country the expense and energy waste of making new bottles and cans. In most states, however, bottle- and can-company lobbyists defeated "bottle bills." So to make money selling your garbage, you have to find a Reynolds Aluminum recycling center. Reynolds now pays 23¢ a pound for used aluminum like old cans and castings from car or lawn-mower transmissions. If you want to collect beer and soft-drink cans, 23¢ a pound averages out to slightly more than a penny a can. Call 800-228-2525 to find the location of a recycling pick-up point near you.

Paper companies are also paying for old cardboard and newspaper. The going rate is now about $1 per 100 pounds. That's a stack of newspapers as high as your waist. This may not sound like big money, but I know a group of high school students who raised $20,000 this way. To find a recycling location, call a local dealer (under "Waste Paper" in the Yellow Pages). You may have to call several dealers because some buy only from companies, not from individuals.

SELLING VALUABLES

Furs, jewelry, antiques, etc., *seem* to be good investments. At least if you try to *buy* them now, they'll cost you far more than they did years ago. *Selling* them for a profit is another matter.

As a test for WCBS-TV News, I tried selling a diamond, some rare books, a used fur coat and an old camera. I got ripped off each time. Why? The first problem is the markup. Many stores that buy and sell valuables have markups of up to 300%, and at a markup of even one-third that size, your valuables would have to double in price before you could break even selling them. To make matters worse, not all dealers offer you the real value of your valuables. I certainly did *not* get a fair shake when I tried to sell the diamond:

I borrowed a $5,000 diamond from a jeweler and had several independent appraisers confirm its $5,000 value. Then I tried to sell it; jewelry experts told me I should have been offered about $3,000. I took it to several jewelry stores and told them that my grandmother had left it to me. One store offered me $2,000, another $1,500 and three dealers in New York City's diamond district offered me only $700.

The following week I returned with a camera crew, identified myself as a reporter, and asked the jewelers, "What would you pay me for it?"

"$3,500," said one.

"$2,500," said another.

Even the ones who had offered only $700 the week before went to $2,700.

I told one jeweler, "When I was here last week, you only offered me $700." He pinched me on the cheek and said, "Oh, that was you! I offered you $2,700."

"Bull," I said and played a tape recording of our original conversation.

"Oh," he replied, "the diamond must have been dusty."

My experiences were similar with the other valuables. One store offered me $20 for a $4,000 mink coat. (The manager claimed it was fake fur.)

The moral: Before you sell, get an expert appraisal (appraisals cost about $25). Don't tell the appraisers that you're planning to sell your valuable or they may give you a lower estimate and then try to buy from you. Instead, tell them you want an appraisal for insurance purposes.

If you go to a jewelry store or market for the appraisal, make sure the expert is familiar with the item you're selling. If it's a jewel, ask the appraiser if he is a qualified gemmologist. Also, look at the stock. Someone who sells Bulova and Seiko watches may not accurately appraise an old enameled watch.

After you get your estimate, visit several stores. Show the buyer the item you wish to sell and your expert appraisal. By comparison shopping you'll get the best price.

WORK AT HOME

I'm sure there are ways to make money while staying at home, but the schemes advertised in most newspapers are total ripoffs. You've seen the ads:

EARN MONEY AT HOME STUFFING ENVELOPES. UP TO $150 A WEEK FULL OR PART TIME. SEND $2 TO BOX 218 . . .

UP TO $30,000 IN SIX WEEKS GUARANTEED OR YOUR MONEY BACK. SEND $12 FOR STARTER KIT. WORK AT HOME.

I recently replied to twenty of these ads. Half the companies kept my money and sent me nothing. Others sent brochures that suggested I run ads like the ones they ran. In other words, I should cheat people in the same way I had been cheated. Another wrote back and said, "Send $2 for moneymaking details!" I did. They wrote back again and said, "Send $15 for moneymaking plans!" I did again. Then they sent me the brochure suggesting I run ads of my own. No one sent me envelopes to stuff.

When I tried confronting the companies I kept finding tiny rooms filled with elderly ladies sorting mail. Were these ladies the ripoff artists? No. They were just making a few dollars an hour working part time. They mailed the money to post-office boxes in Canada. I never could find the crooks who were really behind the schemes.

Of the dozens of "work at home" ads we investigated, we never found *any* that were legitimate moneymakers.

Miscellaneous

This chapter includes advice about buying by mail, shipping things, summer camps, speed reading, and tips on buying shoes, furs, pets, bikes and watches. I don't know how these topics fit in one chapter, but what could I do? Here I am near the end of this book, and I have advice on all these subjects. So here goes.

BUYING BY MAIL—SHIPPING THINGS

Many good products are sold cheaply by mail because the manufacturer doesn't have to maintain stores. It's also good for us because we don't have to drive around to shop.

Often, however, dishonest manufacturers use the mails because not having a store protects them from having to confront irate consumers. When you send away for the MIRACLE WEIGHT LOSS—BURNS AWAY FAT pill and it proves worthless, or doesn't arrive at all, the manufacturer knows you probably can't complain. If you did take the trouble to go the address where you've sent your money (as I've done, cameras rolling), you find three elderly ladies running a mail-sorting operation. They of course don't know anything about the ripoff company: they only mail the companies money.

Just because the company runs a full-page ad in your local newspaper doesn't mean the offer is legitimate. Most newspapers take ads from anybody who pays. Don't count on the postal inspectors to protect you. Sometimes they take action, but they are so slow about it that by the time anything is done, the crook has already changed his business's name, its location, and now is ripping off a new set of people. Nevertheless, there's a chance the postal inspector might help you. Write: Consumer Advocate, U.S. Postal Service, Washington, D.C. 20260.

As for ordering merchandise from legitimate companies, the law says:

They must ship the merchandise to you within thirty days after you order (unless a different date is specifically stated on the order). If they don't make the deadline, they must tell you when they will be able to ship. You may then accept the later shipment or tell them to forget it. If you tell them to forget it, they must send you a refund.

If someone mails you a product you haven't ordered, you can legally keep it, without paying for it.

JUNK MAIL

Many people actually like getting it. I don't. I get lots of it because I'm always sending away to test ripoff schemes, and once you've been identified as a sucker, the sleazo firms sell your name to other sleazo firms. My mail weighs a ton. My postman hates me.

If you want more or less junk mail, write Mail Preference Service, 6 East 43rd Street, New York, New York 10017. They'll send you a form (see following) that allows you to request more junk mail or to be cut off from most mailing lists. Most lists, not all. The smaller companies are not members of Mail Preference Service, and they'll keep sending you stuff.

You don't have to send away for the form. The Direct Mail Marketing Association says if you just photocopy the following chart, and fill out the form, they'll honor your requests.

SHIPPING PACKAGES

When we ship things, we tend to think of the Post Office. I always did, anyway. But there are other ways to ship, and many are cheaper and faster.

Suppose you want to ship a 10-pound package from New York to Los Angeles. At this writing, the Post Office will charge you $5.30. United Parcel Service, a private company (they're in the

CONSUMER APPLICATION MAIL PREFERENCE SERVICE

From (print)_____

Mail to: Mail Preference Service
6 East 43rd Street, New York, NY 10017

Street_____

City & State_____   Zip_____

I have checked the box to indicate my preference . . .

□ I WANT LESS MAIL (REMOVAL.)

Please add my name to the name-removal file. I understand that you will make the name-removal file available to direct mail advertisers for the sole purpose of removing from their mailing lists the names and addresses contained therein.

Others at my address who also want less mail (or variations of my own name by which mail is received) include:

_____

_____

_____

_____

–OR–

□ I WANT TO SHOP BY MAIL (ADD-ON)

I would like to receive information in the mail, especially on the subjects below (circle letter):

A All subjects

B Automobiles, Parts and Accessories

C Books and Magazines

D Charities

E Civic Organizations

F Clothing

G Foods and Cooking

H Gifts

I Grocery Bargains

J Health Foods & Vitamins

K HiFi and Electronics

L Home Furnishings

M Insurance

N Plants, Flowers

O Photography

P Real Estate

R Sewing, Needlework, Arts & Crafts

S Sports, Camping

T Stamps & Coins

U Stocks & Bonds

V Tools & Equipment

W Travel

X Office Supplies

Date_____   Signature_____

White Pages) charges only $4.10, and gives you free insurance to boot. Both will get the package there in about a week, but United Parcel is usually faster. United Parcel may also be less convenient, because they don't have so many branches as the Post Office, and they don't service some places at all. But for $4 extra they'll go to your house and pick up the package, saving you a trip. The Post Office won't do that.

Another example: A 5-pound package New York to Chicago will cost you $2.14 at the Post Office vs. $1.73 by United Parcel.

Funny how it works, isn't it? The U.S. Post Office charges more and loses money; Congress bills us millions to support it. The free enterprise business (United Parcel) does it cheaper and makes a profit. United Parcel's explanation: "Private enterprise is just more efficient than the government. If you know you can't reach into the public till, you cut costs elsewhere." Of course, the Post Office must ship to every tiny town. UPS doesn't have to.

If you're in an extra hurry to ship, there's Federal Express. They ship by air, and guarantee your 10-pound package will get to Los Angeles in 2 days. Post Office airmail costs less, but takes 3 days. Also, Federal Express will pick up the package at your home and give you free insurance; the Post Office will not.

SHIPPING A PACKAGE
New York to Los Angeles

Weight	Post Office	United Parcel Service	Federal Express	Amtrak	Bus (Greyhound & Trailways)
			2 day/1 day		
5 pounds	$ 3.39	$ 2.51	$13.37/25.37	$ 8.25	$12.25
10 pounds	5.34	4.12	18.18/34.17	8.25	12.25
20 pounds	3.52	7.34	27.12/46.09	8.25	18.45
35 pounds	10.06	12.17	39.85/61.00	8.75	31.00
Delivery Service	Yes	Yes	Yes	No	No

For super-fast service the best deal is the Post Office's new "Express Mail." You have to bring the package to the Post Office, and they guarantee delivery by 3 P.M. the next day. If it doesn't make it by then, you get your money back. Express mail is available only if you're mailing to a major city.

For heavy packages, consider shipping by train. Amtrak will charge a fat $8 for shipping that 10-pound package New York to Los Angeles, but a 35-pound package costs only $8.75—a bargain. But with Amtrak, there's no delivery service. Someone has to pick up the package at the station.

Greyhound and Trailways also ship, but they are generally more expensive. They charge $12 to ship 10 pounds to Los Angeles.

SUMMER CAMP

Would you send your child to a baby sitter you've never met? Probably not. Yet most people do just that when it comes time to send the kids away to summer camp.

No doubt, camping is a wonderful experience for children most of the time. But there are plenty of stories of kids who've been killed, injured, molested, or simply neglected while at summer camp.

The fact that the camp belongs to the YMCA, the Boy Scouts, or the Association of Private Camps is no guarantee of safety or quality. The Association of Private Camps and the American Camping Association don't inspect member camps every year, or even every several years. A recommendation from a camp referral service is no guarantee either. Referral services get commissions from camp directors.

Advice: If you don't have recommendations from other parents, the best thing to do is see the camp itself. Camp directors sometimes make their pitch by coming to your house and showing slides of camp activities. This at least allows you to meet and size up the camp director, but it's no guarantee that the camp is as good as the slides make it out to be. Sometimes a camp director shows slides of someone else's camp. Sometimes the camp does not exist at all: some New York area parents paid

$1,200 to send their children to a Massachusetts camp. When the kids got there, they found some camp buildings, but no adult staff. Eventually the kids called their parents.

Anita Kaplan, mother: "When I got to the camp, I found—I could—the toilets had overflooded. The water was not drinkable. The camp director had described in his letter to me an outdoor soda club. That turned out to be a broken Coke machine outside an abandoned building."

Stossel (to audience): Of course, this didn't necessarily bother the children.

Samantha Kaplan, daughter: "I was enjoying myself—you know . . ."

Stossel (to audience): . . . for a while, anyway. Then they ran out of food, and she ended up in the hospital, suffering from dehydration. Parents picked up all the kids after a few days. The New York Attorney General tried to prosecute the camp's owners, but they had disappeared.

The best protection: Visit the camp yourself. If your children are 8 years old or younger, choose a camp where there is at least one counselor for every 6 campers. If your children are older, there should be one counselor for every 8 children.

SPEED READING

"Triple your reading speed!" says the ad. "Read thick novels in an hour!"

Will the course really help you do that? Maybe.

I surveyed speed-reading schools. Most use similar techniques. First, they break your bad habits. For example, many people move their lips while they read. This prevents you from reading faster than you can talk. Once bad habits are broken, the course forces you to speed up by instructing you to follow your finger or a notecard as you move it quickly down the page. The idea is to teach you to read in whole phrases instead of looking at one word at a time. Much of the course is simply practice—training your brain to grasp bigger phrases.

The course *will* improve your reading speed. If you had bad habits to begin with, it's easy to triple your speed, without losing comprehension. The problem is holding on to what you've learned. I contacted 15 graduates of the Evelyn Wood reading course and asked them if they were glad they had taken the course. Nine were. Six were not. All said, yes, their reading speed improved during the course, but they had slowed down since then. Through lack of practice, much of the speed is lost.

The Evelyn Wood course costs about $400. Professors at reading departments of several universities say other schools that cost half that teach you just as well. Of course, Evelyn Wood says she's the best.

SHOES, FURS, PETS, BIKES AND WATCHES

More about products. I haven't given advice on buying clothing because I think it's too complicated. To really detect value differences, you have to be able to recognize fabrics, inspect buttonholes, and then comparison shop from store to store. I think that's more trouble than it's worth. Most of us buy clothing as much for style as durability anyway.

SHOES

Buying shoes is also mostly a matter of taste. Judging quality ("count the number of stitches from the instep to the . . .") is too miserably complicated for me even to think about.

But *when* you buy is important. Shop for shoes in the afternoon. Our feet swell as we walk on them, so they're bigger by afternoon. If you buy in the morning, buy big, or by afternoon your feet will be killing you.

Fit is especially important for children. A foot is made of twenty-six little bones that take twenty years to grow into their proper positions. If you stuff your children's feet into ill-fitting shoes, you'll probably give them foot problems later. That's why its not a good idea to hand down shoes from older to younger children. Since the older child has shaped the shoe already, it might damage the younger child's foot.

If your child hasn't started walking yet, save money by not buying shoes at all. The experts say: Why cramp the feet unnecessarily? Let them go barefoot, or just wear socks.

Surprisingly, children outgrow socks, too. Even socks, if they're too tight, injure growing feet.

Considering what shoes cost these days, you can save a lot of money if you make your shoes last. Three tips:

Rotate your shoes. When you take off your shoes at the end of the day, put them in the closet and wear another pair tomorrow. Studies have found that if you wear different shoes each day, three pairs will last as long as four pairs worn by someone who wears the same pair several days in a row. Why? Shoes need time to rest, to dry out, to resume their normal shape. One full day's rest does that; one night's rest is not enough.

Using a shoe tree helps shoes keep. Wooden shoe trees are better than plastic or metal, because woods absorbs sweat.

If your shoes are made of leather, you want to keep them from drying out (dry leather cracks). Polish and creams retard the cracking, and I'm told creams work better than liquids. The enemy is water, because when water evaporates, leather tends to split. Polishes keep some water off the leather. When your shoes get soaked, dry them off gently, stuff them with tissues or toilet paper, and let them dry in a moderately warm place. Don't put them in the oven or on the radiator or by any direct source of heat.

FUR COATS

I once took a camera crew to Fifth Avenue, stopped people wearing fur coats, and asked:

Stossel: . . . What about the animal?

Woman in Street: When everyone else is freezing, I realize a couple of possums are very sad, but they're keeping me warm, and I'm taking good care of them.

Woman in Street: Oh dear . . . I try not to think about it. I like to think the animal was just lying there dead, and I didn't do anything to it.

If you care about animals, think about this: Minks that make up a mink coat are bred on farms and killed humanely. If you have a possum, fox, lynx, or raccoon coat, the animal you're wearing was probably caught in a trap that snapped shut on its leg. If the animal couldn't bite off its leg to escape, the trap held it in terrible pain until the trapper found it and killed it to make your fur coat.

Moral issues aside, if you do buy: Make sure it fits. Alterations are incredibly expensive.

Examine the leather underneath. It should be flexible, not stiff. If the leather is the same color as the fur, the coat has been dyed.

Most furs sold are mink. A typical mink costs $5,000. You can get fox for $4,000, Raccoon for $2,000, muscrat and squirrel for $1,500, and rabbit for $500.

Still cheaper are "fake" furs, made of synthetic fibers. Today they make fake furs so well they feel almost like real fur.

After you buy, one tip: When the coat gets wet, don't dry it by a radiator. Just shake it, like the animal would, and hang it up to dry slowly.

PETS

Actually, I'm writing only about dogs and cats, because that's what most people own. If you own a more exotic pet, I assume you already have more trouble than I can help you with.

Rich pet, poor pet: Your first decision is whether to buy a purebred or mixed breed. Purebred animals of course are more expensive. The advantages of the purebreds is predictability. If you want a dog that looks more like a lamb than a dog, you can buy a purebred Bedlington terrier and rest assured that when the puppy grows up it will look like a lamb. However, animal experts say differences between breeds' temperaments (Dobermans are vicious . . . Labradors are good with older children) are exaggerated. Most of these qualities come out of a dog's training or environment.

The disadvantage of purebreds (in addition to cost) is that years of breeding in desired traits has bred in some undesirable genetic traits too. For example, purebred Poodles are prone to heart abnormalities. Purebred Dalmatians are more likely to be deaf.

If you do want a purebred animal, I suggest you go to a dog or cat show. That's a great place to windowshop for a breed you might like, and it also gives you an opportunity to meet local breeders. I think it's safer to buy from a local breeder than from a pet store. Pet-store animals have been shipped from who-knows-where, under who-knows-what conditions. Many have minor diseases.

If you don't want a pet with a better bloodline than yours, the choice is easier and cheaper. Look under "Animal Shelters" in the Yellow Pages. Shelters usually have plenty of mixed breeds, and a few purebreds. Some give the pets away; others ask for small donations. If you don't take these pets, they'll probably be killed. The mongrels in animal shelters are likely to be as cute, happy, and healthy as any purebreed you might buy.

Feeding your pet: Pets generally eat better than their owners. Any dog or cat food that is labeled "nutritionally complete" or "complete and balanced diet" or "meets National Research Council requirements" is good food for your pet. Government officials periodically pull samples of these products off the shelves and test them to make sure the contents provide complete nutrition. No one does that with people food.

"All meat" food, despite the bragging in the ads, is not a complete diet for your pet. For a balanced diet, dogs and cats need cereal and other nonmeat nutrients. If you still want to give your pet more meat, be aware that a can that says "beef" contains more beef than a can that says "beef dinner." A "beef flavor" can contain still less beef.

Animal experts say dry pet foods are just as healthful as canned, or "semi-moist" foods. That makes dry foods the smart buy because they are much, much cheaper. The semi-moist stuff costs more than twice as much (for the same nutrient value). Canned food is often 78% water. You pay for water at pet-food prices. Two cautions: (1) If you feed your pet dry food, make sure *you* provide the water; (2) some veterinarians say dry food is bad for male cats. Other veterinarians say that's a myth.

If your dog sniffs haughtily at dry food and insists on his usual tenderloin steaks, let him wait. Veterinarians say dogs will eat whatever you give them if they get hungry enough. No dog has been known to starve itself. Cats are a different story. Some cats *will* starve themselves rather than eat a pet food they don't like.

If you are trying to get your pet to switch foods, do it gradually. Mix some of the new food with the old. Sudden switching may cause diarrhea. Despite the impression the commercials give, your pet has no need for variety in its diet. *You* may want variety, but your pet doesn't care. Any food labeled "nutritionally complete" is all your pet needs.

BICYCLES

Three types are sold these days: 1 speed, 3 speeds, and 10 speeds. Which is best for you depends upon how you plan to ride.

Serious riders buy 10-speeds. These are the lightweight jobs with handlebars that curve downwards. In a way, you pay for the light weight. For every $30 price jump, weight drops about 3 pounds. There are lots of different models, at prices ranging from $150 to $1,000. I suggest you go to a bike store that rents, and try a few out. You want to buy at a bike store anyway (rather than at a department store), because bikes come unassembled. The department store clerk probably hasn't had enough bike experience to do the assembly properly.

Ten-speeds are built for serious riding. The downward curving handlebars force you into a hunched-over position that gets the most power out of your legs. It's uncomfortable at first, and difficult to ride safely. If you plan only casual, weekend riding, buy an "English Racer," or a 3-speed.

Three-speeds: Consider buying a used one. There are plenty of good ones around, collecting dust. Their owners were seduced by 10-speeds. If you do casual riding on flat terrain, 3-speeds are plenty. New ones cost $100 and up. For slightly fancier riding, 5-speeds are also sold. 5- and 3-speed wheels are a little thicker than 10-speed's, so there's more friction, but less chance of a blowout.

One-speed: This is the old, balloon tire, all-steel bike. It's good for running into people, but difficult to pedal very far.

General tips: Most bike shops rent bikes out. If you don't plan a lot of riding, why not just rent? It's a lot cheaper. Even if you do plan to ride a lot, I suggest renting at first. That way you learn what you want. Many people buy bikes with intentions of commuting to work on them, etc. They ride a few weeks, and then get tired of it.

It's most important that the bike fit you correctly. When you straddle the top bar, there should be an inch or two of clearance between the bar and your crotch. "Women's" bikes don't have the top bar, so just try to imagine where it would be.

Test: Walk the bike forward, holding it only by the seat. If it pulls to the left or right, it's out of alignment. Don't buy it.

DIGITAL WATCHES

Digital watches cost from $15 to $500. Which keeps better time? The $15 or the $500 watch? It probably doesn't matter. Texas Instruments, which makes both, says the insides (the time-keeping works of each) are the same. The difference is the packaging. If you just want accurate time, pay less. When you pay more, you pay for the jewelry.

How to Complain

When it all goes wrong, when my advice does you no good, when the product just does not work and the store says, "Tough luck, buddy," what do you do?

You can always complain to one of those government agencies you have so generously supported all these years. The following chart shows who regulates what:

Airlines
> Civil Aeronautics Board
> 1825 Connecticut Avenue, N.W.
> Washington, D.C. 20428
> 202-673-6047

Auto Safety Problems and Recall Questions
> National Highway Traffic Safety Administration
> Department of Transportation
> 400 7th Street, S.W.
> Washington, D.C. 20590
> 800-424-9393

Bank Credit Problems
> Housing and Credit Division
> Department of Justice, Civil Rights Division
> Washington, D.C. 20530
> 202-633-4713

Credit
> Division of Credit Practice
> Bureau of Consumer Protection
> 633 Indiana Building, Indiana Avenue
> Washington, D.C. 20580
> 202-724-1181

False Advertising
>Federal Trade Commission
>6th and Pennsylvania Avenue, N.W.
>Washington, D.C. 20580
>Write. Don't call.

Food, Cosmetics, Medical Devices
>Food and Drug Administration
>5600 Fishers Lane
>Rockville, Maryland 20857
>301-443-3170

Hazardous Working Conditions
>Occupational Safety and Health Administration
>Department of Labor
>200 Constitution Avenue, N.W.
>Washington, D.C. 20210
>Write. Don't call.

Moving
>Interstate Commerce Commission
>Constitution and 12th Street, N.W.
>Washington, D.C. 20423

Race, Religious, or Sex Discrimination
>Fair Housing and Equal Opportunity Hotline
>800-424-8590

Safety of Products
>Consumer Product Safety Commission
>Washington, D.C. 20207
>800-638-8326
>(if you are in Maryland):
>800-492-2937

Warranties
>Public Reference Branch
>Federal Trade Commission
>6th and Pennsylvania Avenue, N.W.
>Washington, D.C. 20580
>202-523-3598

Is it worth taking the time and trouble to contact one of those agencies? Yes and no. I hope you do take the trouble to write, because only through such complaints do these agencies discover patterns of problems. For example, when enough angry people wrote the Transportation Department about blowouts, Firestone 500 tires were ordered recalled. Ideally, your problem will glare up at some dedicated civil servant who'll be outraged enough to follow it through personally.

But don't hold your breath. Most times, your letter will disappear into the bureaucracy, never to be answered.

Your best chance of getting satisfaction is if your complaint falls into some neat bureaucratic category. For example, if you're improperly bumped by an airline, the CAB really will respond to your letter. If your antiques are smashed by your moving company, the ICC probably will get you a cash settlement. Otherwise, I think you're better off complaining to local agencies. Try your city's consumer affairs department, or the Attorney General's office (look under "State Government" in the White Pages).

Try the Better Business Bureau. The Bureau doesn't regulate anybody. It's not, like most people think, a government organization. The Bureau is an association of businesses. The businesses pay dues to support a staff of people who try to keep other businesses honest. Therefore the Bureau has no police rights. It can't force anybody to do anything. Nevertheless, since some businesses care about maintaining a good reputation with the Bureau, getting the Bureau to intervene may get your problem solved. It's worth a try.

So are the following:

Appliances: MACAP stands for Major Appliances Consumer Action Panel. MACAP tries to settle disputes about major appliances. Address: 20 North Wacker Drive, Chicago, Illinois 60606, 312-984-5858.

Auto Problems: AUTOCAP is sponsored by National Automobile Dealers Association. AUTOCAP tries to settle car disputes concerning some new-car dealers. Main Headquarters: 8400 Westpark Drive, McLean, Virginia 22101. Available in 44 cities.

Three of the four American auto companies also have panels that try to arbitrate between dealer and customer:

American Motors: 313-493-2344
Chrysler: 313-956-5970
Ford: 313-337-6950

Furniture: FICAP—Furniture Industry Consumer Panel.
Box 951
High Point, North Carolina 27261
Write. Don't call.

Travel: American Society of Travel Agents; 212-486-0700.

These are industry groups, so they have some bias, but they nevertheless may be helpful in resolving complaints.

Before asking someone else for help, I'd work on the business itself. Businesses want their customers happy; they want you to come back. If you're treated badly by a clerk, complain to the boss. The big honcho is usually more receptive than the lower level employee. Be loud. Be slightly obnoxious. Insist on your rights. Repeat yourself monotonously. If possible, do it in front of other customers. That makes the store want to settle the complaint quickly. They'd rather pay you than lose other business.

If you complain by mail, write to the president of the company. Just call and ask the switchboard, "What is the president's name?" When Joe Schmoe in the complaint department gets a memo from the Top, "What is the problem here and why hasn't this been settled?" it gets faster action. In your letter, let them know you've sent a copy of the complaint to some government agency. The government agency probably won't do anything, but the store may not know that. Letting them know you're hip to which agency regulates them may intimidate them into giving you what you want.

Sometimes, when all fails, the store says, "Tough, I'm not doing anything about your complaint. If you don't like it, sue me." Then you're in trouble.

You can sue, and you might win. But a lawyer almost always costs you more than the complaint is worth. The law in this country has become too fancy, too slow, and too expensive for most of us to use for solving problems. The one exception is Small Claims Court.

SMALL CLAIMS COURT

Here's one place where the consumer really gets a decent break. The wonderful part is that you don't need a lawyer. You get to argue your case yourself. No depositions, motions, objections, postponements, delays, or other lawyerly wonders.

A typical case: A woman says her $800 curtains were ripped by the house painters who painted her living room.

Painter: "They were already ripped."
Woman: "That's not true!"
Painter: "It is so true. We didn't touch them."
Woman: "You ripped my curtains!"
Judge: "Madame, calm down. You'll have your chance to speak."
Woman: "But he's not telling the truth."
Painter: "When we came in, we noticed the rip . . ."

And so on. In this case the judge eventually awarded the woman $250.

It's not difficult to sue in Small Claims Court. You simply go there, tell the clerk what you want to sue about, fill out a form, and pay about $5 to cover the cost of sending a summons to the person you're suing. The summons brings you both into court about a month later, and you get to fight it out.

The judge takes care of the legal amenities. All you have to do is answer questions and tell your side of the story. The store you sue may be represented by a lawyer, but don't let that frighten you. Most times consumers sue, they win.

One disadvantage: This is SMALL Claims Court. Every state has a limit on how much you can sue for. In most states the maximum is about $1,000.

Afterword

Does reading this book make you wonder, "Why haven't I read this information before?" In a free-enterprise system we don't expect companies to reveal disadvantages of their products. We do, however, expect to get the information from the press. Unfortunately, much of the press doesn't provide it. Media executives who wax eloquent about free speech when a politician tries to censor a story are curiously silent when advertisers censor stories. Ideas about products are apparently less deserving of free speech than other ideas.

A national magazine once asked me to write an article about ripoffs. I suggested ten topics, including shampoos. The editor said, "Those are good topics, but don't write about hair and shampoos. We get lots of advertising from shampoo companies. Don't write anything about cigarettes either." Eight million readers depend on this magazine for "consumer advice." They don't get it; nor do they get it from many other magazines.

The *Columbia Journalism Review* reports that in *seven* years, no magazine that accepts cigarette ads printed a major article critical of cigarettes. Dr. Elizabeth Whelan, who writes articles on medical topics for "women's" magazines, says she is under orders "not to write bad things about cigarettes."

Newspaper food pages are filled with puff articles ("New mushroom recipe!"); more useful would be charts comparing local prices (Safeway vs. Foodtown vs. A&P, etc.), but almost no newspapers run such charts. They are afraid of losing supermarket advertising.

Wouldn't magazines like *Modern Bride* be more useful to their readers if instead of encouraging them to spend more ("Don't hesitate to register expensive items"), they also warned brides about wedding ripoffs? "No way," says the editor, not in *Modern Bride.* Articles must be "upbeat" to provide a nice climate for advertising. *Modern Bride* exists to service the advertiser, not the reader. Suggesting not all businesses are wonderful might . . . horrors . . . sell less wedding china.

In Detroit, a newspaper consumer reporter had the nerve to suggest not all auto dealers are honest. Local auto dealers canceled advertising. The newspaper editor said, "I never want to see another article like that," and he dropped the consumer beat.

If you don't want flowers at your funeral, Pittsburgh's newspapers won't let you tell people about it. *The Pittsburgh Press* and *Post-Gazette* refuse to print obituaries that say, "Send no flowers." Why? It might offend florists. Again: protect the advertiser; let readers fend for themselves.

The list goes on. Individual incidents seem minor, but Americans spend millions of dollars on dangerous and unnecessary products because much of the press is afraid to name bad guys. It's prostitution. The press always knocks prostitution, but I think it's less obscene to sell sex than to sell out the truth.

I've had the good fortune to work for people who believe that reporters should report freely about everyone, including advertisers. At CBS, the sales and news sides of the company are kept separate, as they should be. I learn about million-dollar advertising cancellations only at company parties, when ad salespeople come up to me and say, "You jerk! You lost me a three-thousand-dollar commission!" ABC, NBC, WNBC, WNEW, WCCO, *Mother Jones, The Washington Post, The Miami Herald,* and a few others have written frankly about advertisers too. Business would be better off if more reporters did. If the press doesn't give consumers accurate information about products, consumers will demand government get more involved. Then we'll be in *real* trouble.

Index

National Information Bureau,
180
National Research Council, 194
National Supermarket Shopper,
87–88
National Underwriter Co.,
151n.
Natural food, 86
Neo-Synephrine, 108
Nervine, 113
Newcastle disease, 162
New England Merchant Bank,
15
Newspaper ads. *See* Classifieds
Newspapers. *See* Recycling
New York City Department of
Consumer Affairs, 90,
138, 170
New York State Banking De-
partment, 170
New York State Consumer Pro-
tection Board, 71, 93
New York State Health Depart-
ment, 141
New York State Office for the
Aging, 152
New York Telephone (Ma Bell),
71, 72
Nitrites, 86, 87
Noxzema, 122
Nyquil, 111
Nytol, 113

Operations, 139–42, 143
"Organic" food, 86
Otolaryngologists, 139
Ovens. *See* Microwave ovens
Overbooking. *See* Flying

PABA, 125
Packard, Vance, 85, 100
Paper recycling, 182
Pass-Saver, 28–29
Pearl Drops toothpaste, 134
Pensions, 179

Pepsi, 114
Perrier, 102
Pets, 193–95
animal shelters, 194
feeding, 194–95
Phenylpropanolomine, 106, 107
pHisoDerm, 122
PhoneCenter stores (New York
Telephone), 72
Phones. *See* Telephones
Pimples. *See* Acne
Planned Parenthood office, 142
Plaque, 133
Plastic surgery, cosmetic, 119
Playboy, 143
Police Relief Fund, 181
Pond's Cold Cream, 121
Possum fur, 192–93
Postal Service, 127, 184, 186,
188, 189
see also Post Office
Post Office
curbing false ads, 143
see also Postal Service
Pregnancy
at Home Pregnancy Tests,
142–43
see also Abortion
Premiums, insurance, 173
Princeton University, 61
Protein, shampoos, 127
Prudential Insurance, 54
Purebreds, 193

Raccoon fur, 192–93
Radiation
leakage tester, 65
and microwave ovens, 65
sunlamps, 125
RC Cola, 114
Reading. *See* Speed Reading
Real estate agents (realtors).
See House, buying;
House, selling
Realtors. *See* Real estate agents